THE EARLY HISTORY
OF BALLOONING

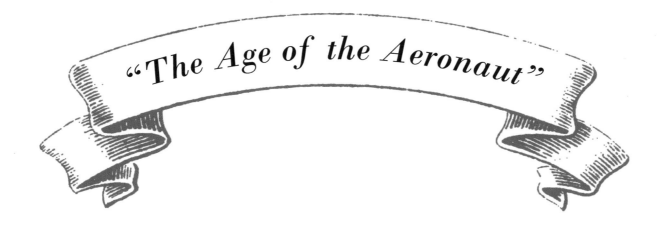

"The Age of the Aeronaut"

Compiled By

Fraser Simons

Compiled by Fraser Simons
Designed by Zoë Horn Haywood
Illustration on Page 24 by Laura Trinder

British Library Cataloguing-in-Publication Data.
A catalogue record for this book is available from the British Library.

THE EARLY HISTORY OF BALLOONING

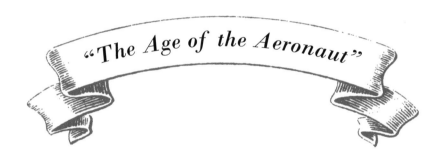

"The Age of the Aeronaut"

CONTENTS

CONTENTS

CHRONOLOGY OF BALLOONING

1783 5th July. The first public demonstration of the hot-air balloon bytheMontgolfier brothers at Annonay, France.

1783 21st November. The Marquis d'Arlandes and Pilâtre de Rozier take part in the first manned voyage in a hot-air balloon.

1783 1st December. Jacques Charles and Nicolas-Louis Robert make the first manned ascent in a hydrogen balloon.

1784 4th June. Madame Thible becomes the first female to ascend in a balloon alongside Mr. Fleurant on 'The Gustave', at Lyon, France.

1784 15th September. Vincenzo Lunardi becomes the first aeronaut to ascend in England.

1785 7th January. The first balloon crossing of the English Channel by Jean-Pierre Blanchard and Dr John Jefferies.

1785 15th June. The first fatal aviation disaster. Pilâtre de Rozier and Pierre Romain die while attempting to cross the English Channel from east to west.

1793   9th January. Blanchard makes the first aerial voyage in the United
States of America.

1797   22nd October. Andrè-Jacques Garnerin's first parachute descent,
at Paris.

1821   19th July. Charles Green's first ascent in a balloon using coal gas.

1836   7th-8th November. A distance of 480 miles is flown by Charles Green
in his "Vauxhall Balloon" from London to Weilburg (Nassau).

1849   15th July. First balloon bombing raid by Austrian forces at the Siege
of Venice.

1861-63   Observation balloons used in the American Civil War.

1870-71   Balloons used to escape the Siege of Paris.

1873   6th October. The first attempt to cross the Atlantic from New York fails.

1897   11th July. S. A. Andrèe leaves Danes Island on his attempt to reach the
North Pole.

INTRODUCTION TO THE EARLY HISTORY OF

Ballooning

In the 21st century – the age of the budget airline – where quick and reliable air travel is available to a large segment of society, it seems hard to comprehend that it is less than 250 years since the first human took to the skies. Throughout history, our species has viewed the birds with wonder, envy, and an irresistible urge for the freedom they possess. Many tried to attain that freedom, and many failed. From the legends of Icarus to the sketches of Leonardo da Vinci, great minds have occupied themselves with replicating the feathered wing – their designs running parallel to the images of heavenly angels in the arts. The principle of creating lift with a wing was of course sound, but it had to wait for the science of the twentieth century to become practical. Until then, a different line of enquiry had to be followed. This spawned the "lighter-than-air period" of aviation.

The concept of heated air being used to generate lift goes back as far as third century C.E. China when Kongming lanterns were used to send messages. It was only in the eighteenth century however, with the innovations of a couple of French paper-makers, the Montgolfier brothers, that the principle was utilised as a means of transport. It was in their balloon, on 21st November 1783, that Pilâtre de Rozier and the Marquis d'Arlandes became the first humans to join the birds and traverse the skies. This ascent was soon followed by that of Charles and Robert in the first hydrogen balloon. The seed had been sown and many others took up the gauntlet to set new records, make scientific observations, and entertain the masses.

In this early-industrial age, the excitement for new technology was immense, and thousands of people would gather and pay to watch these "aeronauts" ascend. The public appetite for all things balloon related led to the coining of the term "Balloonomania", and the enthusiasm for seeing these aviators lift off in their majestic craft is comparable to that of the dawn of the space age in the mid-twentieth century.

As with all forays into the unknown, ballooning took its toll. Several pioneers lost their lives and many more came close. Over the years however, science, and the designs of the balloons became better understood, and although the frontiers of ballooning remain a risky enterprise, many people all over the world now enjoy ballooning as a pastime.

This book contains a collection of writings from some notable chroniclers of aviation history, and along with new content, includes a wealth illustrations and photographs depicting the weird and wonderful early history of ballooning. From the letters of Benjamin Franklin, to the duel fought in balloons, from the Benedictine monk who launched himself off Malmesbury Abbey, to the invention of the airship, I hope the reader is entertained and informed by this miscellany of ballooning history and is inspired to make an ascent themselves.

"Man must rise above the Earth,
to the top of the atmosphere and beyond,
for only thus will he fully understand the
world in which he lives."

– Socrates

THE BALLOONIST'S PRAYER

The winds have welcomed you with softness,
The sun has greeted you with it's warm hands,
You have flown so high and so well,
That God has joined you in laughter,
And set you back gently into
The loving arms of Mother Earth.

— Anon, known as 'The Balloonists Prayer,' believed to have
been adapted from an old Irish sailors' prayer.

TREATS OF EARLY EFFORTS TO FLY, ETCETERA

By R. M. Ballantyne from *Up in the Clouds* (1869)

Before the 'Space Race' and even the Wright brothers, writers were looking back through the history of aviation with fascination and admiration. Though the early ideas were often fanciful, impractical, or down right lethal, it must not be forgotten how the ambition of would-be aviators kept the dream of flight alive. From feathered wings to the copper balloons of Francis Lana, here R. M. Ballantyne (1825-1894) notes the highs and lows of these early attempts at flight.

It is man's nature to soar intellectually, and it seems to have been his ambition from earliest ages to soar physically.

Every one in health knows, or at some period of life must have known, that upward bounding of the spirit which induces a longing for the possession of wings, that the material body might be wafted upwards into those blue realms of light, which are so attractive to the eye and imagination of poor creeping man that he has appropriately styled them the heavens.

Man has envied the birds since the world began. Who has not watched, with something more than admiration, the easy gyrations of the sea-mew, and listened, with something more than delight, to the song of the soaring lark?

To fly with the body as well as with the mind, is a wish so universal that the benignant Creator Himself seems to recognise it in that most attractive passage in Holy Writ, wherein it is said that believers shall "mount up with wings as eagles, they shall run and not be weary, they shall walk and not faint."

Of course man has not reached the middle of the nineteenth century without making numerous attempts to fly bodily up to the skies. Fortunately, however, such ambitious efforts have seldom been made except by the intellectually enthusiastic. Prosaic man, except in the case of the Tower of Babel, has remained content to gaze upwards with longing desire, and only a few of our species in the course

Abbas Ibn Firnas (810-887), a Muslim Berber-Andalusian polymath, is rumoured to have built a glider and made a successful flight in 852. This event is documented by the Moroccan historian Ahmed Mohammed al-Maqqari (d. 1632):

"Among other very curious experiments which he made, one is his trying to fly. He covered himself with feathers for the purpose, attached a couple of wings to his body, and, getting on an eminence, flung himself down into the air, when according to the testimony of several trustworthy writers who witnessed the performance, he flew a considerable distance, as if he had been a bird, but, in alighting again on the place whence he had started, his back was very much hurt, for not knowing that birds when they alight come down upon their tails, he forgot to provide himself with one."

Eilmer of Malmesbury attempted flight from Malmesbury Abbey in the 11th Century. He is purported to have travelled over a furlong (201 metres) before falling and breaking both legs. He also concluded that the failure of the attempt was due to not providing himself with a tail.

of centuries have possessed temerity enough to make the deliberate effort to ride upon the wings of the wind.

Naturally, the first attempts were, like most beginnings, simple and imitative. The birds flew with wings, therefore man put on artificial wings and essayed to fly like the birds. It was not until many grievous disappointments and sad accidents had befallen him, that he unwillingly gave up wings in despair, and set to work to accomplish his ends by more cumbrous and complex machinery.

Very early in the world's history, however, "flying machines" were made, some of which were doubtless intended by their honest inventors to carry men through the air, while others were mere shams, made by designing men, wherewith to impose upon the ignorant for wicked ends of their own; and some of these last were, no doubt, believed to be capable of the feats attributed to them.

The credulity of the ancients is not to be wondered at when we reflect on the magical illusions which science enables us to produce at the present day—illusions so vivid and startling that it requires the most elaborate explanations by adepts and philosophers to convince some among their audiences that what they think they see is absolutely not real! No wonder that the men of old had firm faith in the existence of all kinds of flying machines and creatures.

They believed that fiery dragons were created by infernal machination, which, although not what we may call natural creatures, were nevertheless supposed to rush impetuous through the sky, vomiting flames and scattering the seeds of pestilence far and wide. In those dark ages, writers even ventured to describe the method of imitating the composition of such terrific monsters! A

English Franciscan philosopher and educational reformer Roger Bacon (1214-1294), the first person in the West to give exact directions for making gunpowder, proposed several flying machines. One of these involved a balloon of thin copper sheet that was to be filled with "liquid fire". He thought these balloons would float in the air as light objects do in water. He also investigated the use of mechanical wings in his Treaty of the Admirable Power of Art and Nature, in which he suggests, "to make flying-machines in which the man, being seated or suspended in the middle, might turn some winch or crank, which would put in motion a suit of wings made to strike the air like those of a bird." Although Bacon was a keen advocate of scientific experimentation, it appears that these flying machines remained untested.

number of large hollow reeds were to be bound together, then sheathed completely in skin, and smeared over with pitch and other inflammable matters. This light and bulky engine, when set on fire, launched during thick darkness from some cliff into the air, and borne along by the force of the wind, would undoubtedly carry conviction to the minds of the populace, whilst it would fill them with amazement and terror!

Sometimes, however, those who attempted to practise on the credulity of their fellows were themselves appalled by the results of their contrivances. Such was the case so late as the year 1750, when a small Roman Catholic town in Swabia was almost entirely burnt to ashes by an unsuccessful experiment made by some of the lowest order of priests for the astonishment, if not the edification, of their flocks. An attempt was made by them to represent the effigy of Martin Luther, whom the monks believed to be in league with Satan, under the form of a winged serpent with a forked tail and

Leonardo da Vinci's sketches for a wing design c.1500. Da Vinci produced several such designs for flying contraptions, including an aerial screw machine 96 feet in diameter, built of iron and bamboo framework, and covered with starched linen.

hideous claws. Unfortunately Martin's effigy, when ignited, refused to fly, and, instead of doing what was required of it, fell against the chimney of a house to which it set fire. The flames spread furiously in every direction, and were not subdued until the town was nearly consumed.

In the early part of the sixteenth century a very determined attempt at flying was made by an Italian who visited Scotland, and was patronised by James the Fourth. He gained the favour of that monarch by holding out to him hopes of replenishing his treasury by means of the "philosopher's stone." The wily Italian managed, by his plausible address, to obtain a position which replenished, to some degree, his own empty purse, having been collated by royal favour to the abbacy of Tungland, in Galloway. Being an ingenious fellow, and somewhat, apparently, of an enthusiast, he spent some of his leisure time in fashioning a pair of huge wings of various plumage, with which he actually undertook to fly through the air from the walls of Stirling Castle to France! That he believed himself to be capable of doing so seems probable, from the fact that he actually made the attempt, but fell to the ground with such violence as to break his leg. He was sharp-witted, however, for instead of retiring crest-fallen at his failure, he coolly accounted for the accident by saying, "My wings were composed of various feathers; among them were the feathers of dunghill fowls, and they, by a certain sympathy, were attracted to the dunghill; whereas, had my wings been composed of eagles' feathers alone, the same sympathy would have attracted them to the region of the air!"

It was long before men came to see and admit that in regard to this they were attempting to accomplish the impossible.

There can be no doubt that it is absolutely impossible for man to fly by the simple power of his own muscles, applied to any sort of machinery whatever. This is not an open question. That man may yet contrive to raise himself in the air by means of steam or electricity, or some other motive power, remains to be seen. It does not seem probable, but no one can say authoritatively that it is impossible. It is demonstrable, however, that to rise, or even to remain suspended, in the air by means of machinery impelled by human force alone is a feat which is as much an impossibility as it is

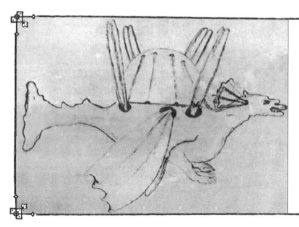

Burattini's Dragon Volant ("Flying Dragon"). This is a sketch of a design by Italian inventor Tio Livio Burattini. In 1647, at the invitation of the Polish King Władysław IV, Burattini built a model of this craft which reportedly successfully lifted a cat.

for a man, by the strength of his own legs, to leap thirty or forty times his own length,—a grasshopper can do that easily, and a bird can fly easily, but a man cannot, and never will be able to do so, because his peculiar conformation forbids it.

This was first demonstrated by Borelli, an eminent Italian mathematician and philosopher, who lived in a fertile age of discovery, and was thoroughly acquainted with the true principles of mechanics and pneumatics. He showed, by accurate calculation, the prodigious force which in birds must be exerted and maintained by the pectoral muscles with which the all-wise Creator has supplied them, and, by applying the same principles to the structure of the human frame, he proved how extremely disproportionate was the strength of the corresponding muscles in man. In fact, the man who should attempt to fly like a bird would be guilty of greater folly and ignorant presumption than the little infant who should endeavour to perform the feats of a gladiator! It is well for man in all things to attain, if possible, to a knowledge of what certainly lies beyond his powers, for such knowledge prevents the waste and misdirection of energies, as well as saving from disappointment and other evil results.

When men began to find that wings refused in any circumstances to waft them to the realms of ether, they set about inventing aerial machines in which to ascend through the clouds and navigate the skies.

In the fourteenth century a glimmering of the true principles on which a balloon could be constructed was entertained by Albert of Saxony, a monk of the order of Saint Augustin, but he never carried his theories into practice. His opinion was that, since fire is more attenuated than air, and floats above the region of our atmosphere, all that was necessary would be to enclose a portion of such ethereal substance in a light hollow globe which would thus be raised to a certain height, and kept suspended in the sky, and that by introducing a portion of air into the globe it would be rendered heavier than before, and might thus be made to descend. This was in fact the statement of the principles on which fire-balloons were afterwards constructed and successfully sent up, excepting that air heated by fire, instead of fire itself, was used.

Giovanni Alfonso Borelli (1608-1679)

Others who came after Albert of Saxony held the same theory, but they all failed to reduce it to practice, and most of these men coupled with their correct notions on the subject, the very erroneous idea that by means of masts, sails, and a rudder, a balloon might be made to sail through the air as a ship sails upon the sea. In this they seem to have confounded two things which are dissimilar, namely, a vessel driven through water, and a vessel floating in air.

It was believed, in those early times, when scientific knowledge was slender, that the dew which falls during the night is of celestial origin, shed by the stars, and drawn by the sun, in the heat of the day, back to its native skies. Many people even went the length of asserting that an egg, filled with the morning dew, would, as the day advanced, rise spontaneously into the air. Indeed one man, named Father Laurus, speaks of this as an observed fact, and gravely gives directions how it is to be accomplished. "Take," says he, "a goose's egg, and having filled it with dew gathered fresh in the morning, expose it to the sun during the hottest part of the day, and it will ascend and rest suspended for a few moments." Father Laurus must surely have omitted to add that a goose's brains in the head of the operator was an element essential to the success of the experiment!

But this man, although very ignorant in regard to the nature of the substances with which he wrought, had some quaint notions in his head. He thought, for instance, that if he were to cram the cavity of an artificial dove with highly condensed air, the imprisoned fluid would impel the machine in the same manner as wind impels a sail. If this should not be found to act effectively, he proposed to apply fire to it in some way or other, and, to prevent the machine from being spirited away altogether by that volatile element, asbestos, or some incombustible material, was to be used as a lining. To feed and support this fire steadily, he suggested a compound of butter, salts, and orpiment, lodged in metallic tubes, which, he imagined, would at the same time heighten the whole effect by emitting a variety of musical tones like an organ!

Another man, still more sanguine than the lest in his aerial flights of fancy, proposed that an ascent should be attempted by the application of fire as in a rocket to an aerial machine. We are not, however, told that this daring spirit ever ventured to try thus to invade the sky.

There can be no doubt that much ingenuity, as well as absurdity, has been displayed in the various suggestions that have been made from time to time,

WILLS'S CIGARETTES.

"FLYING SHIP" of FRANCESCO DE LANA.

A cigarette card from W.D. & H.O Wills, Aviation *series (1910) depicting Francis Lana's flying machine.*

and occasionally carried into practice. One man went the length of describing a huge apparatus, consisting of very long tin pipes, in which air was to be compressed by the vehement action of fire below. In a boat suspended from the machine a man was to sit and direct the whole by the opening and shutting of valves.

Another scheme, more ingenious but not less fallacious, was propounded in 1670 by Francis Lana, a Jesuit, for navigating the air. This plan was to make four copper balls of very large dimensions, yet so extremely thin that, after the air had been extracted, they should become, in a considerable degree, specifically lighter than the surrounding medium. Each of his copper balls was to be about 25 feet in diameter, with the thickness of only the 225th part of an inch, the metal weighing 365 pounds avoirdupois, while the weight of the air which it should contain would be about 670 pounds, leaving, after a vacuum had been formed, an excess of 305 pounds for the power of ascension. The four balls would therefore, it was thought, rise into the air with a combined force of 1220 pounds, which was deemed by Lana to be sufficient to transport a boat completely furnished with masts, sails, oars, and rudders, and carrying several passengers. The method by which the vacuum was to be obtained was by connecting each globe, fitted with a stop-cock, to a tube of at least thirty-five feet long; the whole being filled with water; when raised to the vertical position the water would run out, the stop-cocks would be closed at the proper time, and the vacuum secured. It does not seem to have entered the head of this philosopher that the weight of the surrounding atmosphere would crush and destroy his thin exhausted receivers, but he seems to have been alarmed at the idea of his supposed discovery being applied to improper uses, such as the passing of desperadoes over fortified cities, on which they might rain down fire and destruction from the clouds!Perhaps the grandest of all the fanciful ideas that have been promulgated on this subject was that of Galien, a Dominican friar, who proposed to collect the fine diffused air of the higher regions, where hail is formed, above the summit of the loftiest mountains, and to enclose it in a cubical bag of enormous dimensions—extending more than a mile every way! This vast machine was to be composed of the thickest and strongest sail-cloth, and was expected to be capable of transporting through the air a whole army with all their munitions of war!

There were many other devices which men hit upon, some of which embraced a certain modicum of truth mixed with a large proportion of fallacy. Ignorance, more or less complete, as to the principles and powers with which they dealt, was, in days gone by, the cause of many of the errors and absurdities into which men were led in their efforts to mount the atmosphere.

Laurent de Guzman's Balloon.

"Laurent de Guzman, a monk of Rio Janeiro, performed at Lisbon before the king, John V., raising himself in a balloon to a considerable height. Other versions of the story give a different date, and assign the pretended ascent to 1709. The above engraving, extracted from the "Bibliotheque de la Rue de Richelieu," is an exact copy of Guzman's supposed balloon."

By Fulgence Marion from Wonderful Balloon Ascents (1870).

Unfortunately for Guzman, his ideas were regarded in Rome as heretical and he was seized by officers of the inquisition and thrown in gaol.

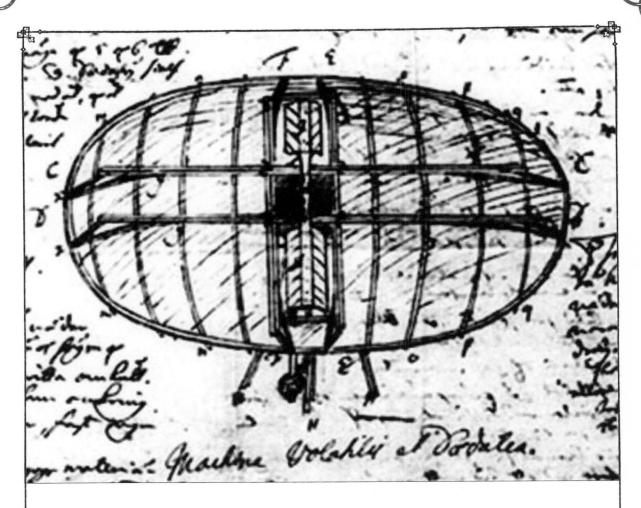

This is a design by Swedish scientist Emanuel Swedenborg in 1714. He did not believe that it would actually fly but thought that it was a good place to start on a problem that would one day be solved.

"It seems easier to talk of such a machine than to put it into actuality, for it requires greater force and less weight than exists in a human body. The science of mechanics might perhaps suggest a means, namely, a strong spiral spring. If these advantages and requisites are observed, perhaps in time to come some one might know how better to utilize our sketch and cause some addition to be made so as to accomplish that which we can only suggest. Yet there are sufficient proofs and examples from nature that such flights can take place without danger, although when the first trials are made you may have to pay for the experience, and not mind an arm or leg."

By Emanuel Swedenborg (1688-1772).

This illustration captures an attempt by the Marquis De Bacqueville, in 1742, to fly across the river Seine from his mansion on the Rue des Saints-Pères, a distance of 600 feet. A huge crowd gathered to watch as the Marquis plummeted on to the deck of a barge, breaking one of his legs in the process. He never repeated the attempt.

An 1885 woodcut of an interesting hybrid of flight designs.

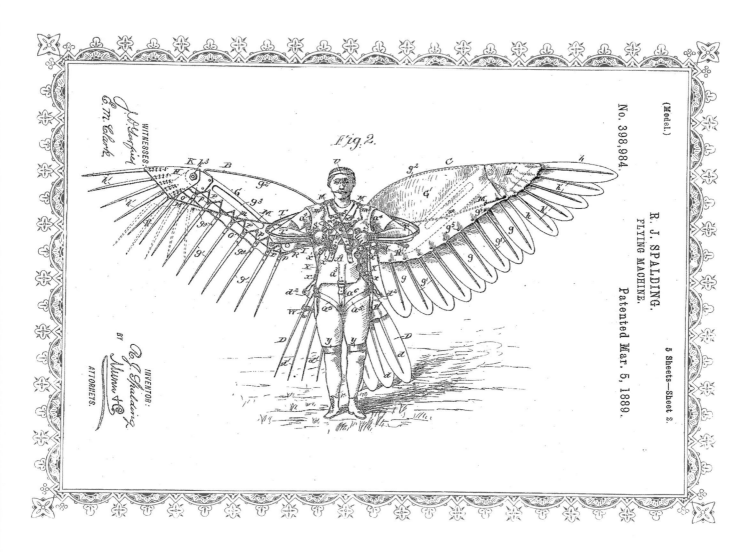

Even as recently as the late 19th century inventors were still designing contraptions to emulate birds. This is U.S. Patent No. 398984, issued March, 5, 1889, for Reuben J. Spaulding's Flying Machine.

THE THEORY OF BALLOONS

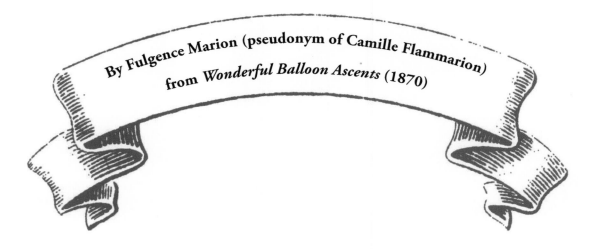

By Fulgence Marion (pseudonym of Camille Flammarion) from *Wonderful Balloon Ascents* (1870)

Camille Flammarion was a French astronomer and prolific author of popular science works about astronomy. He also penned some very early examples of science fiction. Flammarion had a keen interest in the scientific possibilities of ballooning and made many ascents, including several with the celebrated aeronaut Eugène Godard. While aloft, he would make observations of air currents and other meteorological phenomena at different altitudes. As an accomplished author, his accounts of the flights were widely read and he did much to add the popular enthusiasm for ballooning. In the following passage from 1870, Flammarion describes the fundamental physics at the heart of the "lighter-than-air period" of aviation.

A certain proposition in physics, known as the "Principle of Archimedes," runs to the following effect:—"Every body plunged into a liquid loses a portion of its weight equal to the weight of the fluid which it displaces." Everybody has verified this principle, and knows that objects are much lighter in water than out of it; a body plunged into water being acted upon by two forces—its own weight, which tends to sink it, and resistance from below, which tends to bear it up. But this principle applies to gas as well as to liquids—to air as well as to water. When we weigh a body in the air, we do not find its absolute weight, but that weight minus the weight of the air which the body displaces. In order to know the exact weight of an object, it would be necessary to weigh it in a vacuum.

If an object thrown into the air is heavier than the air which it displaces, it descends, and falls upon the earth; if it is of equal weight, it floats without rising or falling; if it is lighter, it rises until it comes to a stratum of air of less weight or density than itself. We all know, of course, that the higher you rise from the earth the density of the air diminishes. The stratum of air that lies upon the surface of the earth is the heaviest, because it supports the pressure of all the other strata that lie above. Thus the lightest strata are the highest.

The principle of the construction of balloons is, therefore, in perfect harmony with physical laws. Balloons are simply globes, made of a light, air-tight material, filled with hot air or hydrogen gas which rise in the air because (they are lighter than the air they displace).

The application of this principle appeared so simple, that at the time when the news of the invention of the balloon was spread abroad the astronomer Lalande wrote—"At this news we all cry, 'This must be! Why did we not think of it before?'" It had been thought of before, but it is often long after an idea is conceived that it is practically realised.

Archimedes of Syracuse (287 BC – c. 212 BC)
Painted by Domenico Fetti

The principle of using hot air to create lift was harnessed as early as the third century C.E. in China. Here, the military strategist and sage, Zhuge Liang (181-234) is reported to have sent up a sky lantern with a message written on it — to summon help when he was surrounded by enemy troops. His courtesy name was Kongming and for this reason they are still known as Kongming lanterns in China. They are now used all over the world at festivals and celebrations.

A Victorian depiction of a legend of a balloon in China in CE 1300. It is supposed to have been flown at the coronation of Empress Fo-Kling.

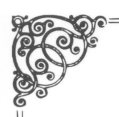

EIGHTEENTH CENTURY SCIENTIFIC PIONEERS

By W. de Fonvielle from *Adventures in the Air* (1877)

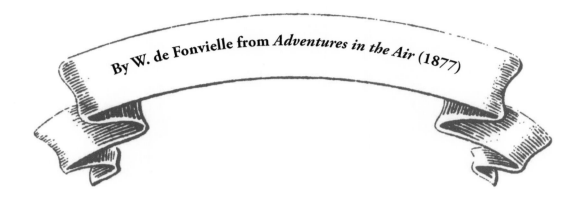

Today, in classrooms all over the world, children are taught the properties of gases and why a balloon ascends, and with this modern education it can be all too tempting, in hindsight, to think that ballooning was an obvious step to take in the development of aviation. However, established knowledge was once at the cutting edge of scientific understanding and it was the observations of trail-blazing scientists that paved the way for the pioneering aeronauts.

The conquest of the air really dates from the memorable day when Galileo told the pump-makers of Florence that nature only abhors a vacuum to the height of thirty-two feet. For the great martyr to science, having exactly ascertained the weight of air, had only to find a lighter body; and if, besides, some means could be devised of holding it fast, mortals might be able to traverse the path- way of the clouds. At one time indeed it might have been thought that the means of mounting aloft had at last been found, when the Burgo-master of Magdeburg, Otto Guericke, discovered the air-pump, by which a hollow sphere may be deprived of all the air it contains. But when he considered the lightness of the mass of air enclosed in his copper globe, and the thickness which must be given to the metal composing the hemispheres to prevent them from being crushed, he must have been devoid of sense to have retained any such illusions. Only fools could imagine, as did the Jesuit Lana, that it would ever be possible to devise any really practicable means of locomotion from an apparatus of a weight so comparatively prodigious. But the discovery of gases, or, as they were called at first, airs, was not long in suggesting to scientific men the invention of balloons. Twenty years before balloons were invented, the scientific principles of aerial navigation were accurately ascertained and published.

In 1766 Cavendish discovered what was then known as "inflammable air," but which we now call hydrogen gas, by the action of sulphuric acid upon metals. He had even learned how to collect it by means of a bladder of gold-beater's skin, as will be seen by a figure which accompanies his Memoir in the "Philosophical Transactions."

Thus the substance which fills balloons and the material of which they are made, had been found out. By a little reflection and investigation it was shown that man had no need of the chimerical wings of Daedalus, since he held in his hands a ship which would enable him to float beyond the clouds. The poets represented the queen of love in a chariot drawn by doves. This graceful myth might well be taken to represent aerial navigation by means of balloons ; but instead of putting bit and bridle upon birds, it is the impalpable spirit, air itself, which is made to draw us along when we have learned how to imprison it. Weight overcomes weight ; a moving force, sufficiently powerful, applied with intelligence, may strive successfully with that powerful but variable and capricious force, which we call the wind.

A prominent name in connection with the early history of ballooning is that of Joseph Black, the eminent professor of chemistry at Edinburgh University towards the end of last century. Black, though of Scotch parentage, was born at Bourdeaux in France in 1728 ; he died in 1799. In the course of his professorial lectures about 1766, Black suggested the idea of raising any weight whatever by attaching it to a large sphere filled with inflammable air, i.e. hydrogen gas, and allowing it to fly off. As Cavendish had determined the specific weight of hydrogen, it was now known that it was as one-thirteenth of the weight of common air. Black went so far as to request Dr. Munro, the professor of anatomy, to give him some thin animal membrane with which to try the experiment, but for some reason or other it seems never to have been made, although it is on record that Black did actually fill a bag with hydrogen that rapidly rose to the ceiling of the room.

Henry Cavendish (1731-1810) was a British natural philosopher and scientist. Along with his discovery of Hydrogen, Cavendish made great contributions to understanding the composition of atmospheric air, the synthesis of water, the mechanical theory of heat, and the law governing electrical attraction and repulsion. He also conducted an experiment to weigh the Earth which has come to be known as "The Cavendish Experiment."

Joseph Black (1728-1799)

From Dr Thomson's *History of Chemistry* (1830)

"Soon after the appearance of Mr Cavendish's paper on hydrogen gas, in which he made an approximation to the specific gravity of that body (showing that it was at least ten times lighter than common air), Dr Black invited a party of friends to supper, informing them that he had a curiosity to show them. Dr Hutton, Mr Clerk of Eldin, and Sir George Clerk of Penicuik, were of the number. When the company had arrived, Dr Black took them into a room where he had the allantois of a calf filled with hydrogen gas, and, upon setting it at liberty, it immediately ascended and adhered to the ceiling. The phenomenon was easily accounted for; it was taken for granted that a small black thread had been attached to the allantois, that the thread passed through the ceiling, and that some one in the apartment above, by pulling the thread, elevated it to the ceiling, and kept it in its position! This explanation was so plausible, that it was agreed to by the whole company, though, like many other plausible theories, it turned out wholly fallacious, for, when the allantois was brought down, no thread whatever was found attached to it. Dr Black explained the cause of the ascent to his admiring friends; but such was his carelessness of his own reputation, that he never gave the least account of this curious experiment even to his class, and several years elapsed before this obvious property of hydrogen gas was applied to the elevation of balloons."

Black's idea was not lost sight of; an accomplished natural philosopher, or physicist, to use the more modern term, who cultivated science in the leisure left him after business, some years later shewed that the thing could be done. This was Tiberius Cavallo, an Italian gentleman settled in London as a merchant. Cavallo, having examined the strong paper used for drawing, thought it would be sufficient to hold the light gas. Indeed he failed to perceive, even by means of a magnifying glass, any pores through which fluid, however subtle, could escape. This substance seemed to him to possess a uniformity of texture and an impermeability which did not belong even to gold-beater's skin. He carefully manufactured some bags into which he put his gas, but through which, alas, his gas escaped. If it had occurred to Cavallo to saturate his bags with oil he would have succeeded admirably. The ingenious Cavallo was not, however, discouraged, but turned his efforts in another direction; he bethought him of collecting his gas in soapy water, such as children are in the habit of using for blowing soap-bubbles. This time the experiment was a complete success; the bubbles which enclosed a portion of the hydrogen gas took flight and rapidly disappeared. This was in 1782.

Tiberius Cavallo (1749-1809)

Thus then the balloon may be said to have been invented. It was necessary, however, to find a solid envelope which would enable it to be utilised, and above all to make it of a size that would remove it from the category of toys. This Cavallo did not attempt. He contented himself with shewing to his colleagues of the Royal Society his beautiful experiment. They all congratulated him on the discovery of a fact so curious, requested him to repeat the experiment at one of the public meetings of the Society, and describe it in their "Transactions." Thus, in England at any rate, the question of aerial navigation did not in the meantime advance beyond soap-bubbles.

But the celebrated Priestley, one of England's greatest scientific worthies and most prolific writers, did not omit to mention so curious a discovery. He described it in terms of high praise in his " Experiments and Observations of the Different Kinds of Airs," which, containing his own discoveries, produced considerable sensation, and was immediately translated into French. Priestley may thus be considered as the link of connection between Cavallo and Montgolfier, a memorable name in the history of ballooning.

THE FRENCH PAPER-MAKER WHO INVENTED THE BALLOON

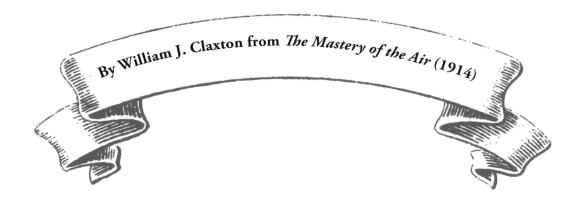

By William J. Claxton from *The Mastery of the Air* (1914)

To this day, the Montgolfier brothers remain the most famous figures in the development of ballooning. It was their imagination and ingenuity that earned them a place in history: being the first to publicly demonstrate the hot-air balloon and Étienne Montgolfier becoming the first man to ascend in one, all be it a tethered model. Their balloon also carried Rozier and d'Arlandes on the first manned free flight on 21st November 1783. From experiments with paper bags to functional flying machines, Joseph and Étienne, the 12th and 15th children respectively of a family of paper manufacturers, turned the aspiration of flight in to a reality. Their name fittingly lives on in the term 'Montgolfière' which continues to be used to refer to a type of balloon that achieves lift with heated air.

In the year 1782 two young Frenchmen might have been seen one winter night sitting over their cottage fire, performing the curious experiment of filling paper bags with smoke, and letting them rise up towards the ceiling. These young men were brothers, named Stephen (Étienne) and Joseph Montgolfier, and their experiments resulted in the invention of the balloon.

The brothers, like all inventors, seem to have had enquiring minds. They were for ever asking the why and the wherefore of things. "Why does smoke rise?" they asked. "Is there not some strange power in the atmosphere which makes the smoke from chimneys and elsewhere rise in opposition to the force of gravity? If so, cannot we discover this power, and apply it to the service of mankind?"

We may imagine that such questions were in the minds of those two French paper-makers, just as similar questions were in the mind of James Watt when he was discovering the power of steam. But one of the most important attributes of an inventor is an infinite capacity for taking pains, together with great patience.

Joseph-Michel Montgolfier   *Jacques-Étienne Montgolfier*

And so we find the two brothers employing their leisure in what to us would, be a childish pastime, the making of paper balloons. The story tells us that their room was filled with smoke, which issued from the windows as though the house were on fire. A neighbour, thinking such was the case, rushed in, but, on being assured that nothing serious was wrong, stayed to watch the tiny balloons rise a little way from the thin tray which contained the fire that made the smoke with which the bags were filled. The experiments were not altogether successful, however, for the bags rarely rose more than a foot or so from the tray. The neighbour suggested that they should fasten the thin tray on to the bottom of the bag, for it was thought that the bags would not ascend higher because the smoke became cool; and if the smoke were imprisoned within the bag much better results would be obtained. This was done, and, to the great joy of the brothers and their visitor, the bag at once rose quickly to the ceiling.

But though they could make the bags rise their great trouble was that they did not know the cause of this ascent. They thought, however, that they were on the eve of some great discovery, and, as events proved, they were not far wrong. For a time they imagined that the fire they had used generated some special gas, and if they could find out the nature of this gas, and the means of making

"A Cloud in a paper bag."

– *Joseph Montgolfier, 1782*

it in large quantities, they would be able to add to their success.

Of course, in the light of modern knowledge, it seems strange that the brothers did not know that the reason the bags rose, was not because of any special gas being used, but owing to the expansion of air under the influence of heat, whereby hot air tends to rise. Every schoolboy above the age of twelve knows that hot air rises upwards in the atmosphere, and that it continues to rise until its temperature has become the same as that of the surrounding air.

The next experiment was to try their bags in the open air. Choosing a calm, fine day, they made a fire similar to that used in their first experiments, and succeeded in making the bag rise nearly 100 feet. Later on, a much larger craft was built, which was equally successful.

It must not be thought that the Montgolfiers experimented solely with hot air in the inflation of their balloons. At one time they used steam, and, later on, the newly-discovered hydrogen gas; but with both these agents they were unsuccessful. It can easily be seen why steam was of no use, when we consider that paper was employed; hydrogen, too, owed its lack of success to the same cause for the porosity of the paper allowed the gas to escape quickly.

It is said that the name "balloon" was given to these paper craft because they resembled in shape a large spherical vessel used in chemistry, which was known by that name. To the brothers Montgolfier belongs the honour of having given the name to this type of aircraft, which, in the two succeeding centuries, became so popular.

An illustration of the statue of the Montgolfier brothers, erected by King Louis XVI, demonstrating the principle of their invention.

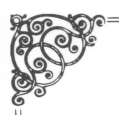

THE FIRST PUBLIC DEMONSTRATION

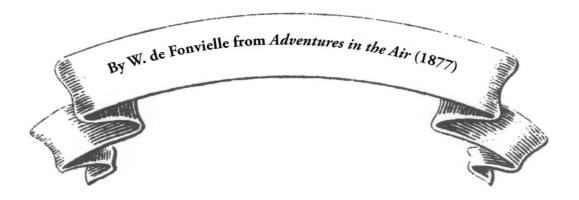

By W. de Fonvielle from *Adventures in the Air* (1877)

Publicly demonstrating their balloon was of the utmost importance to the Montgolfier brothers – being the most effective way of laying claim to their invention. Their balloon made a successful ascent on 5th June 1783, at Annonay, France, in front of a crowd of dignitaries, thus assuring that word that their achievement would travel far and wide.

The first machine which they sent up in the open air had a capacity of 650 cubic feet. It may be said that the first really important attempt surpassed the hopes of the inventors, for the balloon escaped from their hands, like a fiery steed that had escaped from the stable. It came down on the neighbouring hill after having risen to a height estimated at 900 feet This far exceeded the height reached by the most brilliant rockets used in fireworks displays. Having succeeded in this first experiment, the inventor ventured to inflate a much larger machine, one not less than 35 feet in diameter, certainly a great advance on the soap-bubbles of Cavallo. It could raise 450 pounds weight, or nearly 900, including its own weight. This great attempt, which took place on the 3rd April, 1783, was frustrated by the wind; but on the 25th, the experiment was renewed under more favourable atmospheric conditions, and with complete success. The balloon rose and remained suspended in mid air for ten minutes, coming to earth at a distance of 200 feet from the place at which it was let go.

Even at the time when the public press was in its infancy in France, so wonderful an experiment could not long remain unnoticed. The Montgolfiers proposed to M. d'Ormesson, Intendant of the Vivarais to repeat it in presence of the States-General of the province, about to assemble.

The first great public exhibition took place on June 5, 1783. The machine — a linen globe 105 feet in circumference and with a capacity of 23,000 cubic feet — filled with the smoke produced by burning a few handfuls of moist straw, rose quietly and almost majestically to a height of 6000 feet, returning to earth when the gas was dissipated.

1ʳᵉ EXPÉRIENCE AÉROSTATIQUE A ANNONAY le 4 Juin 1783

First public demonstration on 5th June 1783, at Annonay, France. The balloon was made of sackcloth with three thin layers of paper on the inside. It had a capacity of 790 m³ (28,000 cubic feet) and was covered by a reinforcing fish net of cord. It took 1,800 buttons to hold together the four sections constituting the envelope.

AN EYE-WITNESS ACCOUNT

The following passage is an account by Faujas de Saint Fond, French geologist and traveller, on witnessing the Montgolfier's demonstration at Annonay. He took considerable interest in the experiments of the Montgolfier brothers and produced a 2 volume work, Description des expériences de la machine aérostatique de MM. Montgolfier, &c. (1783, 1784), on their achievements. Faujas also produced important works on geology, especially in the study of the origins of volcanoes. The mineral Faujasite is named after him in recognition of his contribution to the field.

"What, was the general astonishment when the inventors of the machine announced that immediately it should be full of gas, which they had the means of producing at will by the most simple process, it would raise itself to the clouds. It must be granted that, in spite of the confidence in the ingenuity and experience of the Montgolfiers, this feat seemed so incredible to those who came to witness it, that the persons who knew most about it—who were, at the same time, the most favourably predisposed in its favour—doubted of its success.

"At last the brothers Montgolfier commenced their work. They first of all began to make the smoke necessary for their experiment. The machine—which at first seemed only a covering of cloth, lined with paper, a sort of sack thirty-five feet high—became inflated, and grew large even under the eyes of the spectator, took consistence, assumed a beautiful form, stretched itself on all sides, and struggled to escape. Meanwhile, strong arms were holding it down until the signal was given, when it loosened itself, and with a rush rose to the height of 1,000 fathoms in less than ten minutes." It then described a horizontal line of 7,200 feet, and as it had lost a considerable amount of gas, it began to descend quietly. It reached the ground in safety; and this first attempt, crowned with such decisive success, secured for ever to the brothers Montgolfier the glory of one of the most astonishing discoveries.

"When we reflect for a moment upon the numberless difficulties which such a bold attempt entailed, upon the bitter criticism to which it would have exposed its projectors had it failed through any accident, and upon the sums that must have been spent in carrying it out, we cannot withhold the highest admiration for the men who conceived the idea and carried it out to such a successful issue."

INVENTIONS & DÉCOUVERTES

Les frères MONTGOLFIER, Joseph (1740-1810) et Étienne (1745-1799) directeurs d'importantes papeteries à Annonay, inventèrent en société le globe aérostatique au moyen de l'air chaud.

Montgolfier Brothers heating a balloon.

SECOND EXPERIMENT

By Fulgence Marion (pseudonym of Camille Flammarion)
from *Wonderful Balloon Ascents* (1870)

Jacques Alexandre César Charles
(1746 –1823)

Charles studied the work of Robert Boyle's 'Boyle's Law', along with that of Henry Cavendish, Joseph Black, and Tiberius Cavallo, and came to the conclusion that hydrogen would be a suitable lifting agent for balloons. This type of balloon came to be known as a 'Charlière' in his honour. He is also recognised for his contribution to the science of gases, in particular their tendency to expand when heated. Although he did not publish his discoveries in this area, in 1802, Joseph Louis Gay-Lussac formulated a scientific law on the subject and named it 'Charles's law' (also known as the law of volumes), crediting it to Charles's unpublished work. During his career, Charles developed several useful inventions, including the hydrometer, reflecting goniometer, a valve to release hydrogen from the balloon, and he improved the Gravesend heliostat and Fahrenheit's aerometer. In 1795, Charles was elected to the Acadèmie des Sciences *and went on to become professor of physics at the Conservatoire des Arts et Métiers. Charles was hot on the heels of the Mongolfier brothers, demonstrating his hydrogen balloon only a couple of months after their ascent at Annonay. The passage below, by Camille Flammarion, describes the demonstration of Charles's balloon that took place at Champ de Mars, Paris, on 27th of August 1783.*

The indescribable enthusiasm caused by the ascent of the first balloon at Annonay, spread in all directions, and excited the wondering curiosity of the savants of the capital. An official report had been prepared, and sent to the Academy of Sciences in Paris, and the result was that the Academy named a commission of inquiry. But fame, more rapid than scientific commissions, and more enthusiastic than academies, had, at a single flight, passed from Annonay to Paris, and kindled the anxious ardour of the lovers of science in that city. The great desire was to rival Montgolfier, although neither the report nor the letters from Annonay had made mention of the kind of gas used by that experimenter to inflate his balloon. By one of the frequent coincidences in the history of the sciences, hydrogen gas had been discovered six years previously by the great English physician Cavendish, and it had hardly even been tested in the laboratories of the chemists when it all at once became famous. A young man well versed in physics, Professor Charles, assisted by two practical men, the brothers Robert, threw himself ardently into the investigation of the modes of inflating balloons with this gas, which was then called INFLAMMABLE AIR. Guessing that it was much lighter than that which Montgolfier had been obliged to make use of in his third-rate provincial town, Charles leagued himself with his two assistants to constrict a balloon of taffeta, twelve feet in diameter, covered with india-rubber, and to inflate it with hydrogen.

The thing thus arranged, a subscription was opened. The projected experiment having been talked of all over Paris, every one was struck with the idea, and subscriptions poured in. Even the most illustrious names are to be found in the list, which may be called the first national subscription in France. Nothing had been written of the forthcoming event in any public paper, yet all Paris seemed to flock to contribute to the curious experiment.

The inflation with hydrogen was effected in a very curious manner. As much as 1,125 lbs. of iron and 560 lbs. of sulphuric acid were found necessary to inflate a balloon which had scarcely a lifting power of 22 lbs., and the process of filling took no less than four hours. At length, however, at the end of the fourth hour, the balloon, composed of strips of silk, coated with varnish, floated, two-thirds full, from the workshop of the brothers Robert.

On the morning of the 26th of August, the day before the ascent was to be made, the balloon was visited at daybreak, and found to be in a promising state. At two o'clock on the following morning its constructors began to make preparations to transport it to the Champ de Mars, from which place it was to be let loose. Skilled workmen were employed in its removal, and every precaution was taken that the gas with which it was charged should not be allowed to escape. In the meantime the excitement of the people about this wonderful structure was rising to the highest pitch. The wagon on which it was placed for removal was surrounded on all sides by eager multitudes, and the night-patrols, both of horse and foot, which were set to guard the avenues leading to where it lay, were quite unable to stem the tide of human beings that poured along to get a glimpse of it.

The conveyance of the balloon to the Champ de Mars was a most singular spectacle. A vanguard, with lighted torches, preceded it; it was surrounded by special attendants, and was followed by detachments of night-patrols on foot and mounted. The size and shape of this structure, which was escorted with such pomp and precaution—the silence that prevailed—the unearthly hour, all helped to give an air of mystery to the proceedings. At last, having passed through the principal thoroughfares, it arrived at the Champ de Mars, where it was placed in an enclosure prepared for its reception.

When the dawn came, and the balloon had been fixed in its place by cords, attached around its middle and fixed to iron rings planted in the earth, the final process of inflation began.

The Champ de Mars was guarded by troops, and the avenues were also guarded on all sides. As the day wore on an immense crowd covered the open space, and every advantageous spot in the neighborhood was crowded with people. At five o'clock the report of a cannon announced to the multitudes, and to scientific men who were posted on elevations to make observations of the great event, that the grand moment had come. The cords were withdrawn, and, to the vast delight and wonder of the crowd assembled, the balloon shot up with such rapidity that in two minutes it had ascended 488 fathoms. At this height it was lost in a cloud for an instant, and, reappearing, rose to a great height, and was again lost in higher clouds. The ascent was a splendid success. The rain that fell damped neither the balloon nor the ardor of the spectators.

This balloon was 12 feet in diameter, 38 feet in circumference, and had a capacity of 943 cubic feet. The weight of the materials of which it was constructed was 25 lbs., and the force of ascension was that of 35 lbs.

The fall of the balloon was caused by the expansion and consequent explosion of the hydrogen gas. This event took place some distance out in the country, close to a number of peasants, whose terror at the sight and the sound of this strange monster from the skies was beyond description. The people assembled, and two monks having told them that the burst balloon was the hide of a monstrous animal, they immediately began to assail it vigorously with stones, flails, and pitchforks. The cure of the parish was obliged to walk up to the balloon to reassure his terrified flock. They finally attached the burst envelope to a horse's tail, and dragged it far across the fields.

Many drawings and engravings of the period represent the peasants armed with pitchforks, flails, and scythes, assailing it, a dog snapping at it, a garde-champetre firing at it, a fat priest preaching at it, and a troop of young people throwing stones at the unfortunate machine.

The news of this fiasco came to Paris, but too late. When search was made for the covering, scarcely a fragment could be found.

A somewhat humorous result of all this was the issue of a communication from government to the people, entitled, "Warning to the People on kidnapping Air-balloons." This document, duly signed and approved of, describes the ascents at Annonay and at Paris, explains the nature and the causes of the phenomena, and warns the people not to be alarmed when they see something like a "black moon" in the sky, nor to give way to fear, as the seeming monster is nothing more than a bag of silk filled with gas.

This first ascent in Paris was an important event. Every one, from the smallest to the greatest, was deeply interested in it, while to the man of science it was one of the most exciting of incidents. For the purpose of observing the altitude to which the balloon rose, and the course it took, Le Gentil was on the observatory, Prevost was on one of the towers of Notre Dame, Jeaurat was on La Place Louis XV., and d'Agelet was on the Champ de Mars. It was only Lalande that frowned as he witnessed the success of the experiment. He had predicted the year before that air-navigation was impossible.

When Charles's balloon finally reached the ground it is said to have been attacked by peasants with pitchforks. Apparently they were scared of this strange, foul-smelling, hissing creature. Hydrogen itself is odourless but the process used to create it involved pouring sulphuric acid over iron shavings. It was a less than perfect method which resulted in a stench similar to that of rotten eggs.

Benjamin Franklin (1706-1790)

FRANKLIN ON THE FIRST HYDROGEN BALLOON

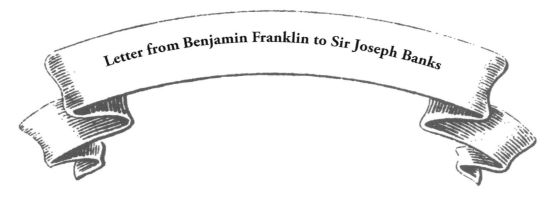

Letter from Benjamin Franklin to Sir Joseph Banks

This is a letter written by Benjamin Franklin, polymath and Founding Father of the United States, while he was Minister to the Court of France. He had a keen interest in the invention of the balloon and is writing here to Sir Joseph Banks, President of the Royal Society of London, to inform him of the latest developments in the race to master the skies.

Passy, Aug. 30, 1783.

Sir,

On Wednesday, the 27th Instant the new aerostatic Experiment, invented by Messrs. Montgolfier, of Annonay, was repeated by M. Charles, Professor of experimental Philosophy at Paris.

A hollow Globe 12 feet Diameter was formed of what is called in England Oiled Silk, here Taffetas gommé, the Silk being impregnated with a Solution of Gum elastic in Lintseed Oil, as is said. The Parts were sewed together while wet with the Gum, and some of it was afterwards passed over the Seams, to render it as tight as possible.

It was afterwards filled with the inflammable Air that is produced by pouring Oil of Vitriol upon Filings of Iron, when it was found to have a tendency upwards so strong as to be capable of lifting a Weight of 39 Pounds, exclusive of its own Weight which was 25 lbs. and the Weight of the Air contain'd.

It was brought early in the morning to the Champ de Mars, a Field in which

Reviews are sometimes made, lying between the Military School and the River. There it was held down by a Cord till 5 in the afternoon, when it was to be let loose. Care was taken before the Hour to replace what Portion had been lost, of the inflammable Air, or of its Force, by injecting more.

It is supposed that not less than 50,000 People were assembled to see the Experiment. The Champ de Mars being surrounded by Multitudes, and vast Numbers on the opposite Side of the River.

At 5 aClock Notice was given to the Spectators by the Firing of two Cannon, that the Cord was about to be cut. And presently the Globe was seen to rise, and that as fast as a Body of 12 feet Diameter, with a force only of 39 Pounds, could be suppos'd to move the resisting Air out of its Way. There was some Wind, but not very strong. A little Rain had wet it, so that it shone, and made an agreeable Appearance. It diminished in Apparent Magnitude as it rose, till it enter'd the Clouds, when it seem'd to me scarce bigger than an Orange, and soon after became invisible, the Clouds concealing it.

The Multitude separated, all well satisfied and delighted with the Success of the Experiment, and amusing one another with discourses of the various uses it may possibly be apply'd to, among which many were very extravagant. But possibly it may pave the Way to some Discoveries in Natural Philosophy of which at present we have no Conception.

A Note secur'd from the Weather had been affix'd to the Globe, signifying the Time & Place of its Departure, and praying those who might happen to find it, to send an account of its State to certain Persons at Paris. No News was heard of it till the next Day, when Information was receiv'd, that it fell a little after 6 aClock, at Gonesse, a Place about 4 Leagues Distance, and that it was rent open, and some say had Ice in it. It is suppos'd to have burst by the Elasticity of the contain'd Air when no longer compress'd by so heavy an Atmosphere.

One of 38 feet Diameter is preparing by Mr. Montgolfier himself, at the Expence of the Academy, which is to go up in a few Days. I am told it is constructed of Linen & Paper, and is to be filled with a different Air, not yet made Public, but cheaper than that produc'd by the Oil of Vitriol, of which 200 Paris Pints were consum'd in filling the other.

It is said that for some Days after its being filled, the Ball was found to lose an eighth Part of its Force of Levity in 24 Hours; Whether this was from Imperfection in the Tightness of the Ball, or a Change in the Nature of the Air, Experiments may easily discover.

I thought it my Duty, Sir, to send an early Account of this extraordinary Fact, to the Society which does me the honour to reckon me among its Members; and I will endeavour to make it more perfect, as I receive farther Information.

With great Respect, I am, Sir, Your most obedient and most humble Servant

B. FRANKLIN

P. S. Since writing the above, I am favour'd with your kind Letter of the 25th. I am much obliged to you for the Care you have taken to forward the Transactions, as well as to the Council for so readily ordering them on Application. Please to accept and present my Thanks.

I just now learn, that some observers say, the Ball was 150 Seconds in rising, from the Cutting of the Cord till hid in the Clouds; that its height was then about 500 Toises, but, being moved out of the Perpendicular by the Wind, it had made a Slant so as to form a Triangle, whose Base on the Earth was about 200 Toises. It is said the Country People who saw it fall were frightned, conceiv'd from its bounding a little, when it touched the Ground, that there was some living Animal in it, and attack'd it with Stones and Knives, so that it was much mangled; but it is now brought to Town and will be repaired.

The great one of M. Montgolfier, is to go up, as is said, from Versailles, in about 8 or 10 Days; It is not a Globe but of a different Form, more convenient for penetrating the Air. It contains 50,000 cubic Feet, and is supposed to have Force of Levity equal to 1500 pounds weight. A Philosopher here, M. Pilatre du Rozier has seriously apply'd to the Academy for leave to go up with it, in order to make some Experiments. He was complimented on his Zeal and Courage for the Promotion of Science, but advis'd to wait till the management of these Balls was made by Experience more certain & safe. They say the filling of it in M. Montgolfier's Way will not cost more than half a Crown. One is talk'd of to be 110 feet Diameter. Several Gentlemen have ordered small ones to be made for their Amusement. One has ordered four of 15 feet Diameter each; I know not with what Purpose; But such is the present Enthusiasm for promoting and improving this Discovery, that probably we shall soon make considerable Progress in the art of constructing and using the Machines.

Among the Pleasanteries Conversation produces on this Subject, some suppose Flying to be now invented, and that since Men may be supported in the Air, nothing is wanted but some light handy Instruments to give and direct Motion. Some think Progressive Motion on the Earth may be advanc'd by it, and that a Running Footman or a Horse slung and suspended under such a Globe so as to have no more of Weight pressing the Earth with their Feet, than Perhaps 8 or 10 Pounds, might with a fair Wind run in a straight Line across Countries as fast as that Wind, and over Hedges, Ditches & even Waters. It has been even fancied that in time People will keep such Globes anchored in the Air, to which by Pullies they may draw up Game to be preserved in the Cool & Water to be frozen when Ice is wanted. And that to get Money, it will be contrived to give People an extensive View of the Country, by running them up in an Elbow Chair a Mile high for a Guinea &c. &c.

B. F.

First aerial voyage by Charles and Robert.

THE VERSAILLES BALLOON

By R. M. Ballantyne from *Up in the Clouds* (1869)

The competition to engineer the best flying machine focussed the efforts of Charles and the Montgolfier brothers and caused a quick succession of 'aviation firsts'. The next ballooning milestone was that of sending living creatures up into the atmosphere, a feat that was to be achieved by a Montgolfier Balloon at Versailles in September 1783.

The Parisians now appeared to become balloon-mad. The Royal Academy of Sciences invited Joseph Montgolfier to repeat his experiments, and another balloon was prepared by him of coarse linen with a paper lining, which, however, was destroyed by incessant and violent rain before it could be tried. Undeterred by this, another was constructed by him, which ascended from Versailles on the 19th of September 1783.

This balloon deserves peculiar notice as being the first which carried up living creatures. A sheep, a cockerel, and a duck, were the first aeronauts! They ascended to a height of about 1500 feet; remained suspended for a time, and descended some two miles off in perfect safety—indeed we may say in perfect comfort, for the sheep was discovered to be quietly feeding when it returned to the earth!

Aérostat Réveillon ascent from Versailles on 19th September 1783. The passengers, a sheep, a duck, and a cockerel were chosen for scientific reasons: the sheep as a rough approximation of human physiology, the duck as a control for the effects created by the aircraft and not the altitude, and the cockerel as a further control being a bird that did not fly at altitude.

THE FIRST MAN TO ASCEND IN A BALLOON

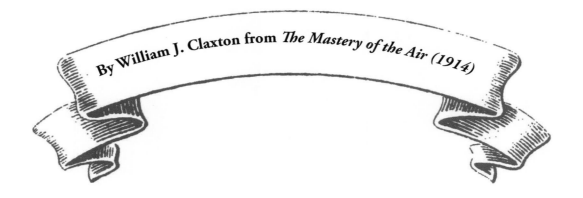

By William J. Claxton from *The Mastery of the Air (1914)*

After thousands of years dreaming of taking to the skies, it was on 21st November 1783 that the human race finally became airborne. In a balloon constructed by the Montgolfiers, in collaboration with Jean-Baptiste Réveillon, a French wall-paper manufacturer, Pilâtre de Rozier and the marquis d'Arlandes ascended from Paris as the first aeronauts (successfully petitioning King Louis XVI for the honour after the King decreed that condemned criminals would be the first to ascend due to the risk involved). The balloon was as majestic as the occasion required, with Rèvellion adding the rich decorative touches to wow the crowds. It was beautifully adorned with gold figures of signs of the zodiac and suns with Louis XVI's face in the centres, all set on a deep blue background. Though not completely uneventful, the voyage was an unparalleled success and ushered in the dawn of manned flight.

The safe descent of the three animals, which has already been related, showed the way for man to venture up in a balloon. In our time we marvel at the daring of modern airmen, who ascend to giddy heights, and, as it were, engage in mortal combat with the demons of the air. But, courageous though these deeds are, they are not more so than those of the pioneers of ballooning.

In the eighteenth century nothing was known definitely of the conditions of the upper regions of the air, where, indeed, no human being had ever been; and though the frail Montgolfier balloons had ascended and descended with no outward happenings, yet none could tell what might be the risk to life in committing oneself to an ascent. There was, too, very special danger in making an ascent in a hot-air balloon. Underneath the huge envelope was suspended a brazier, so that the fabric of the balloon was in great danger of catching fire.

It was at first suggested that two French criminals under sentence of death should be sent up, and, if they made a safe descent, then the way would be open for other aeronauts to venture aloft. But everyone interested in aeronautics in those days saw that the man who first traversed the unexplored

*Jean-François
Pilâtre de Rozier
(1754-1785)
was a chemistry and
physics teacher, and an
aeronautical pioneer.*

*François Laurent
le Vieux d'Arlandes
(1742–1809)*

regions of the air would be held in high honour, and it seemed hardly right that this honour should fall to criminals. At any rate this was the view of M. Pilatre de Rozier, a French gentleman, and he determined himself to make the pioneer ascent.

De Rozier had no false notion of the risks he was prepared to run, and he superintended with the greatest care the construction of his balloon. It was of enormous size, with a cage slung underneath the brazier for heating the air. Before making his free ascent De Rozier made a trial ascent with the balloon held captive by a long rope.

At length, in November, 1783, accompanied by the Marquis d'Arlandes as a passenger, he determined to venture. The experiment aroused immense excitement all over France, and a large concourse of people were gathered together on the outskirts of Paris to witness the risky feat. The balloon made a perfect ascent, and quickly reached a height of about half a mile above sea-level. A strong current of air in the upper regions caused the balloon to take an opposite direction from that intended, and the aeronauts drifted right over Paris. It would have gone hard with them if they had been forced to descend in the city, but the craft was driven by the wind to some distance beyond the suburbs and they alighted quite safely about six miles from their starting-point, after having been up in the air for about half an hour.

Their voyage, however, had by no means been free from anxiety. We are told that the fabric of the balloon repeatedly caught fire, which it took the aeronauts all their time to extinguish. At times, too, they came down perilously near to the Seine, or to the housetops of Paris, but after the most exciting half-hour of their lives they found themselves once more on Mother Earth.

FIGURE EXACTE   ET PROPORTIONS.

DU GLOBE   AËROSTATIQUE,

Qui, le premier,   a enlevé

des Hommes   dans les Airs.

Hauteur du Globe...........70. pieds   ‖   Poids du Globe...........1600.Liv.

Diametre...............46. pieds   ‖   Poids qu'il à enlevé 16. à 1700 Liv.

Capacité........60000.pieds cubes   ‖   La Gallerie avoit 3. pieds de largeur.

La partie superieure étoit entourée de Fleurs-de-lys; au-dessous les 12 Signes du Zodiaque.
Au milieu les Chiffres du Roi, entremêlés de Soleils.
Le bas, étoit garni de Mascarons et de Guirlandes; plusieurs Aigles à ailes éployées
paroissoient suporter en l'air cette puissante Machine.
Tous ces ornemens étoient de couleur d'or sur un beau fond bleu, ensorte que ce superbe Globe paroissoit être d'or et d'azur.
La Gallerie circulaire, dans laquelle on voyoit M. le Marquis D'ARLANDES et
M. PILATRE DE ROZIER, étoit peinte en Draperies cramoisi à franges d'or.

A beautiful illustration from 1786, of the balloon that carried Rozier and d'Arlandes. They reached an altitude of about 3,000 feet and travelled for a distance of 9 kilometres.

Lift off !

MAKING HISTORY

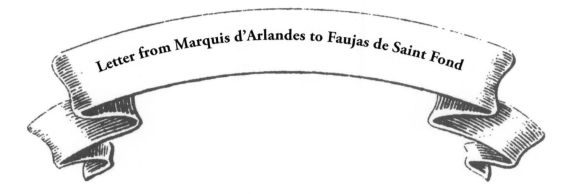

Letter from Marquis d'Arlandes to Faujas de Saint Fond

The following passage is from a letter written by the Marquis d'Arlandes to Faujas de Saint Fond describing the first manned ascent in a balloon. Full of admiration for the expertise of Rozier, d'Arlande presents a very gentlemanly account of this historic voyage.

I wish to describe as well as I can the first journey which men have attempted through an element which, prior to the discovery of the Messieurs Montgolfier, seemed so little fitted to support him.

We went up on the 21st of November, 1783, at near two o'clock. M. Rozier on the west side of the balloon, I on the east. The wind was nearly north-west. The machine, say the public, rose with majesty; but really the position of the balloon altered so that M. Rozier was in the advance of our position, I in the rear.

I was surprised at the silence and the absence of movement which our departure caused among the spectators, and believed them to be astonished and perhaps awed at the strange spectacle; they might well have reassured themselves. I was still gazing when M. Rozier cried to me, "You are doing nothing, and the balloon is scarcely rising a fathom."

"Pardon me," I answered, as I placed a bundle of straw upon the fire and slightly stirred it. Then I turned quickly but already we had passed out of sight of La Muette. Astonished I cast a glance towards the river. I perceived the confluence of the Oise. And naming the principal bends of the river by the places nearest them, I cried, "Passy, St. Germain, St. Denis, Sevres!"

"If you look at the river in that fashion you will be likely to bathe in it soon," cried Rozier. "Some fire, my dear friend, some fire!"

First manned voyage. Illustration from the late 19th Century.

We traveled on; but instead of crossing the river, as our direction seemed to indicate, we bore towards the Invalides, them returned upon the principal bend of the river, and traveled to above the barrier of La Conference, thus dodging about the river, but not crossing it.

"The river is very difficult to cross," I remarked to my companion.

"So it seems," he answered; "but you are doing nothing. I suppose it is because you are braver than I, and don't fear a tumble."

I stirred the fire; I seized a truss of straw with my fork; I raised it and threw it in the midst of the flames. An instant afterwards I felt myself lifted as if it were into the heavens.

"For once we move," said I.

"Yes, we move," answered my companion.

At the same instant I heard from the top of the balloon a sound which made me believe that it had burst. I watched, yet I saw nothing. My companion had gone into the interior, no doubt to make some observations. As my eyes were fixed on the top of the machine I experienced a shock, and it was the only one I had yet felt. The direction of the movement was from above, downwards. I then said "what are you doing? Are you having a dance to yourself"

"I'm not moving."

"So much the better. It is only a new current which I hope will carry us from the river," I answered. I turned to see where we were, and found we were between the Ecole Militaire and the Invalides.

"We are getting on," said Rozier.

"Yes, we are travelling."

"Let us work, let us work," said he.

I now heard another report in the machine, which I believed was produced by the cracking of a cord. This new intimation made me carefully examine the inside of our habitation. I saw that the part that was turned towards the south was full of holes, some of which were of a considerable size.

"It must descend," I then cried.

"Why?"

"Look!" I said. At the same time I took my sponge and quietly extinguished the fire that was burning some of the holes within my reach; but at the same moment I perceived that the bottom of the cloth was coming away from the circle which surrounded it.

"We must descend," I repeated to my companion. He looked below. "We are upon Paris," he said. "It does not matter," I answered. "Only look! is there no danger? Are you holding on well" "Yes."

I examined from my side, and saw that I had nothing to fear. I then tried with my sponge the ropes which were within my reach. All of them held firm. Only two of the cords had broken. I then said, "We can cross Paris."

During this operation we were rapidly getting down to the roofs. We made more fire, and rose again with the greatest ease. I looked down, and it seemed to me we were going towards the towers of St. Sulpice; but, on rising, a new current made us quit this direction and bear more to the south. I looked to the left, and beheld a wood, which I believed to be that of the Luxembourg. We were traversing the boulevard, and I cried all at once "Get to the ground!"

But the intrepid Rozier, who never lost his head, and who judged more surely than I, prevented me from attempting to descend. I then threw a bundle of straw on the fire. We rose again, and another current bore us to the left. We were now close to the ground, between two mills. As soon as we came near the earth I raised myself over the gallery, and leaning there with my two hands, I felt the balloon pressing softly against my head. I pushed it back, and leaped to the ground. Looking round and expecting to so see the balloon still distended, I was astonished to find it quite empty and flattened. On looking for Rozier I saw him in his shirt-sleeves creeping from under the mass of canvas that had fallen over him. Before attempting to descend he had put off his coat and placed it in the basket. After a deal of trouble we were at last all right.

As Roziers was without a coat I besought him to go to the nearest house. On his way thither he encountered the Duke of Chartres, who had followed us, as we saw, very closely, for I had had the honour of conversing with him the moment before we set out.

"We now know a method of mounting into the air, and I think we are not likely to know more. The vehicles can serve no use till we can guide them; and they can gratify no curiosity till we mount with them to greater heights than we can reach without; till we rise above the tops of the highest mountains, which we have yet not done. We know the state of the air in all its regions, to the top of Teneriffe, and, therefore, learn nothing from those who navigate a balloon below the clouds. The first experiment, however, was bold, and deserves applause and reward. But since it has been performed, and its event is known, I had rather now find a medicine that can ease an asthma."

– Dr. Samuel Johnson, in a letter to Dr. Brocklesby, 6 October 1784.

THE SECOND AERIAL VOYAGE

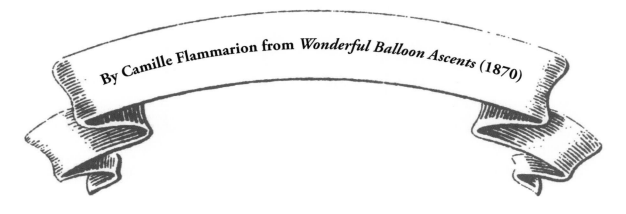

By Camille Flammarion from *Wonderful Balloon Ascents* (1870)

The first manned voyage had been accomplished only days earlier and the public appetite for balloons was at fever pitch when hundreds of thousands of people amassed, and paid, to watch professor Charles and Nicolas-Louis Robert make the first ascent in a hydrogen balloon, from Paris on 1st December 1783. There was plenty of rivalry between the supporters of the Montgolfier brothers and those of professor Charles, but in a wonderful example of sportsmanship, Charles honoured Joseph Montgolfier by asking him to release the small pilot balloon used to assess the conditions. Like the first voyage, this ascent also had its share of peril, so much so in fact that Charles never went up in a balloon again. The following passage contains Charles's account of the voyage and goes some way to explaining why he might have decided to abandon his career as an aeronaut.

The first ascent of Roziers and Arlandes was a feat of hardihood almost unique. The men's courage was, so to speak, their only guarantee. Thanks to the balloon, however, they accomplished one of the most extraordinary enterprises ever achieved by our race.

On the day after the experiment of the Champ de Mars (27th of August), Professor Charles—who had already acquired celebrity at the Louvre, by his scientific collection and by his rank as an official instructor—and the Brothers Robert, mechanicians, were engaged in the construction of a balloon, to be inflated with hydrogen gas, and destined to carry a car and one or two passengers. For this ascent Charles may be said to have created all at once the art of aerostation as now practiced, for he brought it at one bound to such perfection that since his day scarcely any advance has been made upon his arrangements. His simple yet complete invention was that of the valve which gives escape to the hydrogen gas, and thus renders the descent of the balloon gentle and gradual; the car that carries the travellers; the ballast of sand, by which the ascent is regulated and the fall is moderated; the coating of caoutchouc, by means of which the material of the balloon is rendered airtight and

An illustration of Professor Jacques Charles and Nicolas-Louis Robert ascending in the first manned hydrogen balloon flight on 1st December 1783, from the Jardin des Tulieries in Paris.

A contemporary illustration of the first manned flight in a hydrogen balloon.

prevents loss of gas; and, finally, the use of the barometer, which marks at every instant, by the elevation or the depression of the mercury, the position in which the aeronaut finds himself in the atmosphere. Charles created all the contrivances, or, in other words, all the ingenious precautions which make up the art of aerostation.

On the 26th of November, the balloon, fitted with its network, and having the car attached to it, was sent away from the hall of the Tuileries, where it had been exhibited. The ascent was fixed for the 1st of December, 1783, a memorable day for the Parisians.

At noon upon that day, the subscribers, who had paid four louis for their seats, took their places within the enclosure outside the circle, in which stood the casks employed for making the gas. The humbler subscribers, at three francs a-head, occupied the rest of the garden. The number of spectators, as we read underneath the numerous coloured prints which represent this spectacle, was 600,000; but though, without doubt, the gardens of the Tuileries are very large, it is probable this figure is a considerable overstatement, for this number would have been three-fourths of the whole population of Paris.

The roofs and windows of the houses were crowded, whilst the Pont Royal and the square of Louis XV. were covered by an immense multitude. About mid-day a rumour was spread to the effect that the king forbade the ascent. Charles ran to the Chief Minister of State, and plainly told him that his life was the king's, but his honour was his own: his word was pledged to the country and he would ascend. Taking this high ground, the bold professor gained an unwilling permission to carry out his undertaking.

A little afterwards the sound of cannon was heard. This was the signal which announced the last arrangements and thus dissipated all doubt as to the rising of the balloon. There had during the day been considerable disturbance among the crowd, between the partisans of Charles and Montgolfier; each party extolled its hero, and did everything possible to detract from the merits of the rival inventor. But whatever ill-feeling might have existed was swept away by Professor Charles with a compliment. When he was ready to ascend, he walked up to Montgolfier, and, with the true instinct of French politeness, presented him with a little balloon, saying at the same time—

"It is for you, monsieur, to show us the way to the skies."

The exquisite taste and delicacy of this incident touched the bystanders as with an electric shock, and the place at once rang out with the most genuine and hearty applause The little balloon thrown up by Montgolfier sped away to the north-east, its beautiful emerald colour showing to fine effect in the sun.

From this point let us follow the narrative of Professor Charles himself.

"The balloon," he says, "which escaped from the hands of M. Montgolfier, rose into the air, and seemed to carry with it the testimony of friendship and regard between that gentleman and myself, while acclamations followed it. Meanwhile, we hastily prepared for departure. The stormy weather did not permit us to have at our command all the arrangements which we had contemplated the previous evening; to do so would have detained us too long upon the earth. After the balloon and the car were in equilibrium, we threw over 19 lbs. of ballast, and we rose in the midst of silence, arising from the emotion and surprise felt on all sides.

"Nothing will ever equal that moment of joyous excitement which filled my whole being when I felt myself flying away from the earth. It was not mere pleasure; it was perfect bliss. Escaped from the frightful torments of persecution and of calumny, I felt that I was answering all in rising above all.

"To this sentiment succeeded one more lively still—the admiration of the majestic spectacle that spread itself out before us. On whatever side we looked, all was glorious; a cloudless sky above, a most delicious view around. 'Oh, my friend,' said I to M. Robert, 'how great is our good fortune! I care not what may be the condition of the earth; it is the sky that is for me now. What serenity! what a ravishing scene! Would that I could bring here the last of our detractors, and say to the wretch, Behold what you would have lost had you arrested the progress of science.'

"Whilst we were rising with a progressively increasing speed, we waved our bannerets in token of our cheerfulness, and in order to give confidence to those below who took an interest in our fate. M. Robert made an inventory of our stores; our friends had stocked our commissariat as for a long voyage—champagne and other wines, garments of fur and other articles of clothing.

"'Good,' I said; 'throw that out of the window.' He took a blanket and launched it into the air, through which it floated down slowly, and fell upon the dome of l'Assomption.

"When the barometer had fallen 26 inches, we ceased to ascend. We were up at an elevation of 1,800 feet. This was the height to which I had promised myself to ascend; and, in fact, from this moment to the time when we disappeared from the eyes of our friends, we always kept a horizontal course, the barometer registering 26 inches to 26 inches 8 lines.

"We required to throw over ballast in proportion as the almost insensible escape of the hydrogen gas caused us to descend, in order to remain as nearly as possible at the same elevation. If circumstances had permitted us to measure the amount of ballast we threw over, our course would have been almost absolutely horizontal.

"After remaining for a few moments stationary, our car I changed its course, and we were carried on at the will of the wind. Soon we passed the Seine, between St. Ouen and Asnieres. We traversed the river a second time, leaving Argenteuil upon the left. We passed Sannois, Franconville, Eau-Bonne, St. Leu-Taverny, Villiers, and finally, Nesles. This was about twenty-seven miles from Paris, and we had reached this distance in two hours, although there was so little wind that the air scarcely stirred.

"During the whole course of this delightful voyage, not the slightest apprehension for our fate or that of our machine entered my head for a moment. The globe did not suffer any alteration beyond the successive changes of dilatation and compression, which enabled us to mount and descend at will. The thermometer was, during more than an hour, between ten and twelve degrees above zero; this being to some extent accounted for by the fact that the interior of the car was warmed by the rays of the sun.

"At the end of fifty-six minutes, we heard the report of the cannon which informed us that we

An illustration of the filling of a hydrogen balloon.

had, at that moment, disappeared from view at Paris. We rejoiced that we had escaped, as we were no longer obliged to observe a horizontal course, and to regulate the balloon for that purpose.

"We gave ourselves up to the contemplation of the views which the immense stretch of country beneath us presented. From that time, though we had no opportunity of conversing with the inhabitants, we saw them running after us from all parts; we heard their cries, their exclamations of solicitude, and knew their alarm and admiration.

"We cried, 'Vive le Roi!' and the people responded. We heard, very distinctly—'My good friends, have you no fear? Are you not sick? How beautiful it is! Heaven preserve you! Adieu, my friends.'

"I was touched to tears by this tender and true interest which our appearance had called forth.

"We continued to wave our flags without cessation, and we perceived that these signals greatly increased the cheerfulness and calmed the solicitude of the people below. Often we descended sufficiently low to hear what they shouted to us. They asked us where we came from, and at what hour we had started.

"We threw over successively frock-coats, muffs, and habits. Sailing on above the Ile d'Adam, after having admired the splendid view, we made signals with our flags, and demanded news of the Prince of Conti. One cried up to us, in a very powerful voice, that he was at Paris, and that he was ill. We regretted missing such an opportunity of paying our respects, for we could have descended into the prince's gardens, if we had wished, but we preferred to pursue our course, and we re-ascended. Finally, we arrived at the plain of Nesles.

"We saw from the distance groups of peasants, who ran on before us across the fields. 'Let us go,' I said, and we descended towards a vast meadow.

"Some shrubs and trees stood round its border. Our car advanced majestically in a long inclined plane. On arriving near the trees, I feared that their branches might damage the car, so I threw over two pounds of ballast, and we rose again. We ran along more than 120 feet, at a distance of one or two feet from the ground, and had the appearance of travelling in a sledge. The peasants ran after us without being able to catch us, like children pursuing a butterfly in the fields.

"Finally, we stopped, and were instantly surrounded. Nothing could equal the simple and tender regard of the country people, their admiration, and their lively emotion.

"I called at once for the cures and the magistrates. They came round me on all sides: there was quite a fete on the spot. I prepared a short report, which the cures and the syndics signed. Then arrived a company of horsemen at a gallop. These were the Duke of Chartres, the Duke of Fitzjames, and M. Farrer. By a very singular chance, we had come down close by the hunting-lodge of the latter. He leaped from his horse and threw himself into my arms, crying, 'Monsieur Charles, I was first!'

"Charles adds that they were covered with the caresses of the prince, who embraced both of them. He briefly narrated to the Duke of Chartres some incidents of the voyage.

"'But this is not all, monseigneur. I am going away again,' added Charles.

"'What! Going away!' exclaimed the duke.

"'Monseigneur, you will see. When do you wish me to come back again?' I said.

Jacques Alexandre César Charles departing at Nesle, France, after landing the first hydrogen balloon flight from Paris.

"'In half an hour.'

"'Very well: be it so. In half an hour I shall be with you again.'

"M. Robert descended from the car, and I was alone in the balloon.

"I said to the duke, 'Monseigneur, I go.' I said to the peasants who held down the balloon, 'My friends, go away, all of you, from the car at the moment I give the signal.' I then rose like a bird, and in ten minutes I was more than 3,000 feet above the ground. I no longer perceived terrestrial objects; I only saw the great masses of nature.

"In going away, Charles had taken his precautions against the possible explosion of the balloon, and made himself ready to make certain observations. In order to observe the barometer and the thermometer, placed at different extremities of the car, without endangering the equilibrium, he sat down in the middle, a watch and paper in his left hand, a pen and the cord of the safety-valve in his right.

"I waited for what should happen," continues he. "The balloon, which was quite flabby and soft when I ascended, was now taut, and fully distended. Soon the hydrogen gas began to escape in considerable quantities by the neck of the balloon, and then, from time to time, I pulled open the valve to give it two issues at once; and I continued thus to mount upwards, all the time losing the inflammable air, which, rushing past me from the neck of the balloon, felt like a warm cloud.

"I passed in ten minutes from the temperature of spring to that of winter; the cold was keen and dry, but not insupportable. I examined all my sensations calmly; *I* COULD HEAR MYSELF LIVE, so to speak, and I am certain that at first I experienced nothing disagreeable in this sudden passage from one temperature to another.

"When the barometer ceased to move I noted very exactly eighteen inches ten lines. This observation is perfectly accurate The mercury did not suffer any sensible movement.

"At the end of some minutes the cold caught my fingers; I could hardly hold the pen, but I no longer had need to do so. I was stationary, or rather moved only in a horizontal direction.

"I raised myself in the middle of the car, and abandoned myself to the spectacle before me. At my departure from the meadow the sun had sunk to the people of the valleys; soon he shone for me alone, and came again to pour his rays upon the balloon and the car. I was the only creature in the horizon in sunshine—all the rest of nature was in shade. Ere long, however, the sun disappeared, and thus I had the pleasure of seeing him set twice in the same day. I contemplated for some moments the mists and vapours that rose from the valley and the rivers The clouds seemed to come forth from the earth, and to accumulate the one upon the other. Their colour was a monotonous grey—a natural effect, for there was no light save that of the moon.

"I observed that I had tacked round twice, and I felt currents which called me to my senses. I found with surprise the effect of the wind, and saw the cloth of my flag: extended horizontally.

"In the midst of the inexpressible pleasure of this state of ecstatic contemplation, I was recalled to myself by a most extraordinary pain which I felt in the interior of the ears and in the maxillary glands. This I attributed to the dilation of the air contained in the cellular tissue of the organ as much as to the cold outside. I was in my vest, with my head uncovered. I immediately covered my head with a bonnet of wool which was at my feet, but the pain only disappeared with my descent to the ground.

"It was now seven or eight minutes since I had arrived at this elevation, and I now commenced to descend. I remembered the promise I had made to the Duke of Chartres, to return in half an hour. I quickened my descent by opening the valve from time to time. Soon the balloon, empty now to one half, presented the appearance of a hemisphere.

"Arrived at twenty-three fathoms from the earth, I suddenly threw over two or three pounds of ballast, which arrested my descent, and which I had carefully kept for this purpose. I then slowly descended upon the ground, which I had, so to speak, chosen."

Such is the narrative of the second aerial voyage. After such a memorable ascent one is astonished to learn that Professor Charles never repeated his experiment. It has been said that, in descending from his car, he had vowed that he would never again expose himself to such perils, so strong had been the alarm he felt when the peasants ceasing to hold him down he shot up into the sky with the rapidity of an arrow. But after him a thousand others have followed the daring example he set. With this ascent the memorable year 1783 closed, and the seed which had been sown soon began to be productive.

Monsieur Charles and the Duke of Chartres.

FRANKLIN ON THE SECOND AERIAL VOYAGE BY MAN

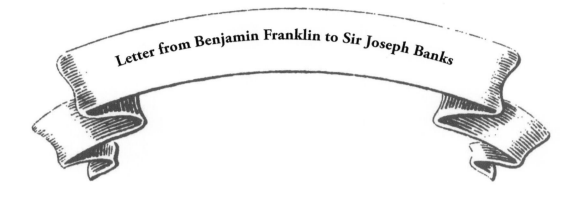

Letter from Benjamin Franklin to Sir Joseph Banks

This is another letter written by Benjamin Franklin in which he gives a spectator's account of the first manned ascent in a hydrogen balloon.

Passy, Dec. 1, 1783.

Dear Sir,

In mine of yesterday, I promis'd to give you an Account of Mess[rs]. Charles & Robert's Experiment, which was to have been made at this Day, and at which I intended to be present. Being a little indispos'd, & the Air cool, and the Ground damp, I declin'd going into the Garden of the Tuilleries where the Balloon was plac'd, not knowing how long I might be oblig'd to wait there before it was ready to depart; and chose to stay in my Carriage near the Statue of Louis XV. from whence I could well see it rise, & have an extensive View of the Region of Air thro' which, as the Wind sat, it was likely to pass. The Morning was foggy, but about one aClock, the Air became tolerably clear, to the great Satisfaction of the Spectators, who were infinite, Notice having been given of the intended Experiment several Days before in the Papers, so that all Paris was out, either about the Tuilleries, on the Quays & Bridges, in the Fields, the Streets, at the Windows, or on the Tops of Houses, besides the Inhabitants of all the Towns & Villages of the Environs.

Never before was a philosophical Experiment so magnificently attended. Some Guns were fired to give Notice, that the Departure of the great Balloon was near, and a small one was discharg'd which went to an amazing Height, there being but little Wind to make it deviate from its perpendicular Course, and at length the Sight of it was lost. Means were used, I am told, to prevent the great Balloon's rising so high as might indanger its Bursting. Several Bags of Sand were taken on board before the Cord that held it down was cut, and the whole Weight being then too much to be lifted, such a Quantity was discharg'd as to permit its Rising slowly. Thus it would sooner arrive at that Region where it would be in Equilibrio with the surrounding Air, and by discharging more Sand afterwards, it might go higher if desired. Between One & Two aClock, all Eyes were gratified with seeing it rise majestically from among the Trees, and ascend gradually above the Buildings, a most beautiful Spectacle! When it was about 200 feet high, the brave Adventurers held out and wav'd a little white Pennant, on both Sides their Car, to salute the Spectators, who return'd loud Claps of Applause. The Wind was very little, so that the Object, tho' moving to the Northward, continued long in View; and it was a great while before the admiring People began to disperse. The Persons embark'd were Mr. Charles, Professor of Experimental Philosophy, & a zealous Promoter of that Science; and one of the Messieurs Robert, the very ingenious Constructors of the Machine. When it arrived at its height, which I suppose might be 3 or 400 Toises, it appeared to have only horizontal Motion. I had a Pocket Glass, with which I follow'd it, till I lost Sight, first of the Men, then of the Car, and when I last saw the Balloon, it appear'd no bigger than a Walnut. I write this at 7 in the Evening. What became of them is not yet known here. I hope they descended by Day-light, so as to see & avoid falling among Trees or on Houses, and that the Experiment was completed without any mischievous Accident which the Novelty of it & the want of Experience might well occasion. I am the more anxious for the Event, because I am not well inform'd of the Means provided for letting themselves gently down, and the Loss of these very ingenious Men would not only be a Discouragement to the Progress of the Art, but be a sensible Loss to Science and Society.

I shall inclose one of the Tickets of Admission, on which the Globe was represented, as originally intended, but is altered by the Pen to show its real State when it went off. When the Tickets were engraved, the Car was to have been hung to the Neck of the Globe, as represented by a little Drawing I have made in the Corner A. I suppose it may have been an Apprehension of Danger in straining too much the Balloon or tearing the Silk, that induc'd the Constructors to throw a Net over it, fix'd to a Hoop which went round its Middle, and to hang the Car to that Hoop, as you see in Fig. B.

Tuesday Morning, Dec. 2. I am reliev'd from my Anxiety, by hearing that the Adventurers descended well near l'Isle Adam, before Sunset. This Place is near 7 Leagues from Paris. Had the Wind blown fresh, they might have gone much farther.

If I receive any farther Particulars of Importance I shall communicate them hereafter.

With great Esteem, I am, Dear Sir, Your most obedient & most humble servant,

B. FRANKLIN

P. S. Tuesday Evening.

Since writing the above, I have receiv'd the printed Paper & the Manuscript, containing some Particulars of the Experiment, which I enclose.—I hear farther, that the Travellers had perfect Command of their Carriage, descending as they pleas'd by letting some of the inflammable Air escape, and rising again by discharging some Sand; that they descended over a Field so low as to talk with Labourers in passing and mounted again to pass a Hill. The little Balloon falling at Vincennes, shows that mounting higher it met with a Current of Air in a contrary Direction: An Observation that may be of use to future aerial Voyagers.

"How posterity will laugh at us, one way or other! If half a dozen break their necks, and balloonism is exploded, we shall be called fools for having imagined it could be brought to use: if it should be turned to account, we shall be ridiculed for having doubted."

— *Horace Walpole, letter to Horace Mann, 24 June 1785*

Whichever type of balloon used, inflation could be fraught with danger. This print
is of a failed attempt to inflate a balloon in 1784 by Abbé Miolan and Janinet.

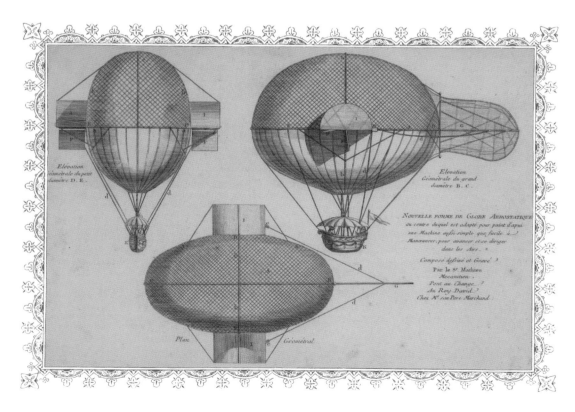

An early design for a balloon with steering capability (1784).

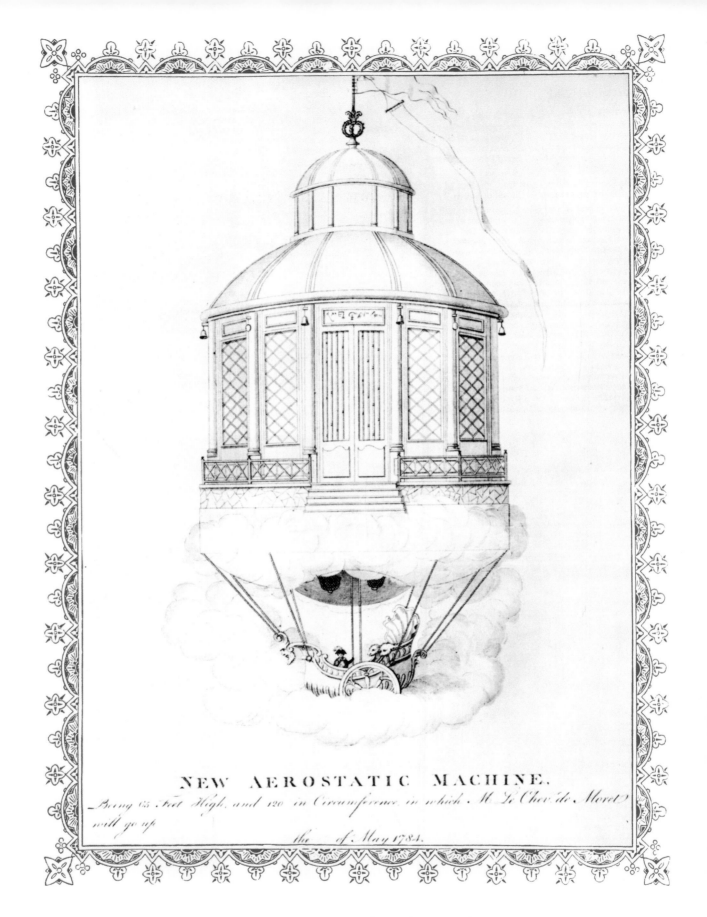

NEW AEROSTATIC MACHINE,

Being 65 Feet High, and 120 in Circumference, in which M. Le Chev.de Morel will go up the of May 1784.

A rather extravagant design from 1784.

A design by Richard Crosbie, this machine was built and exhibited in Dublin in 1784. Although an interesting concept, it never made a successful ascent.

JEAN-PIERRE BLANCHARD

Jean-Pierre Blanchard (1753-1809) was a French inventor and celebrated aeronaut. From an early age he invented a variety of interesting contraptions, including a velocipede, a rat trap that involved a pistol, and a hydraulic pump system that raised water from the Seine to Chateau Gaillard (a height of 122 metres). He also undertook many attempts at designing flying machines, though none were successful. The engraving below of his counterpoise is an example of one of these efforts. The two pulleys were suspended from a tall mast, and with a 20 pound counterpoise on one side, and Blanchard on the other, he would power the parachute like wings with the action of his arms and legs. He is reported to have lifted himself eighty feet in the air, but all he had really done was lifted the weight of his body minus that of the counterpoise. Once the Montgolfier brothers demonstrated their balloon in 1783 however, Blanchard realised the problem of lift was solved and turned his attention to becoming an aeronaut. He attempted to invent many improvements to the balloon, such as adding flapping wings, oars, and windmills, but none proved effective.

Although Blanchard's inventions did not aid balloon flight, he made a great contribution to the field by publicising the technology around the world. He holds the records for the first balloon flights in Belgium, Germany, the Netherlands, Poland, and America, as well as the record for the first crossing of the English Channel. His flight in the United States was even witnessed by the country's first President, George Washington.

Unfortunately, in 1808, Blanchard suffered a heart attack during an ascent and fell from his balloon. Although he survived the fall, he died a year later from the severe injuries he sustained.

His wife, Sophie Blanchard, who had made many ascents with him, continued to support herself with ballooning and became the most celebrated female aeronaut in Europe.

Jean-Pierre Blanchard
(1753-1809)

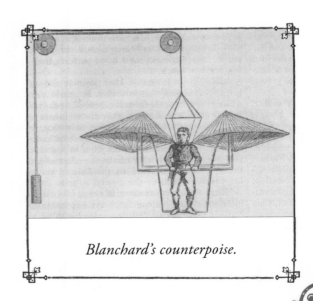

Blanchard's counterpoise.

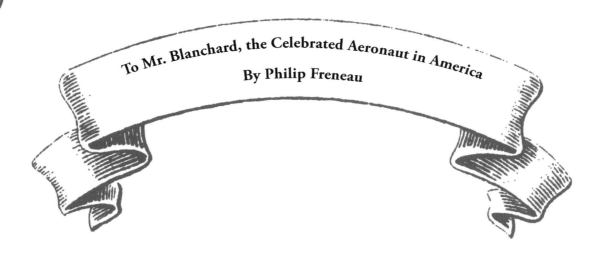

To Mr. Blanchard, the Celebrated Aeronaut in America
By Philip Freneau

The exploits of Blanchard in the United States inspired this poem by Philip Freneau (1752-1832). Freneau was an American poet, nationalist, polemicist, sea captain, and newspaper editor. He is sometimes called the "Poet of the American Revolution."

Nil mortalibus ardui est

Caelum ipsum petimus stultitia

— Horace

FROM Persian looms the silk he wove
No Weaver meant should trail above
The surface of the earth we tread,
To deck the matron or the maid.

But you ambitious, have design'd
With silk to soar above mankind:--
On silk you hang your splendid car
And mount towards the morning star.

How can you be so careless--gay:
Would you amidst red lightnings play;
Meet sulphurous blasts, and fear them not--
Is Phaeton's sad fate forgot?

Beyond our view you mean to rise--
And this Balloon, of mighty size,
Will to the astonish'd eye appear,
An atom wafted thro' the air.

Where would you rove? amidst the storms,

Departed Ghosts, and shadowy forms,
Vast tracks of aether, and, what's more,
A sea of space without a shore!--

   Would you to Herschell find the way--
To Saturn's moons, undaunted stray;
Or, wafted on a silken wing,
Alight on Saturn's double ring?

   Would you the lunar mountains trace,
Or in her flight fair Venus chase;
Would you, like her, perform the tour
Of sixty thousand miles an hour?--

   To move at such a dreadful rate
He must propel, who did create--
By him, indeed, are wonders done
Who follows Venus round the sun.

   At Mars arriv'd, what would you see!--
Strange forms, I guess--not such as we;
Alarming shapes, yet seen by none;
For every planet has its own.

   If onward still, you urge your flight
You may approach some satellite,
Some of the shining train above
That circle round the orb of Jove.

Attracted by so huge a sphere
You might become a stranger here:
There you might be, if there you fly,
A giant sixty fathoms high.

May heaven preserve you from that fate!
Here, men are men of little weight:
There, Polypheme, it might be shown,
Is but a middle sized baboon.--

This ramble through, the aether pass'd,
Pray tell us when you stop at last;
Would you with gods that aether share,
Or dine on atmospheric air?--

You have a longing for the skies,
To leave the fogs that round us rise,
To haste your flight and speed your wings
Beyond this world of little things.

Your silken project is too great;
Stay here, Blanchard, 'till death or fate
To which, yourself, like us, must bow,
Shall send you where you want to go.

Yes--wait, and let the heav'ns decide;--
Your wishes may be gratified,
And you shall go, as swift as thought,
Where nature has more finely wrought,

Her Chrystal spheres, her heavens serene;
A more sublime, enchanting scene
Than thought depicts or poets feign.

CHANNEL CROSSING

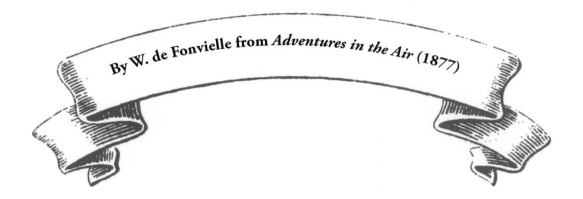

By W. de Fonvielle from *Adventures in the Air* (1877)

The ambition of the aeronautical pioneers was only matched by their bravery and it was not long before their attention was focussed on setting new records. Blanchard, with a keen eye for showmanship and theatre, realised that crossing the English Channel would be a feat worthy of recognition, and on 7th January 1785, he set off with Dr. Jefferies from Dover, England, and successfully landed in Guînes, France, about 2½ hours later. Their courage was handsomely rewarded, as you will see from this passage by W. de Fonvielle.

On January 7th, 1785, at 1 p.m., Blanchard ascended in a balloon from Dover Castle. He had with him Dr. J. Jeffries, an American physician. Two hours after the time of ascent, the two reached the earth in the forest of Guines. Twice while crossing the Channel the balloon descended, and, to save themselves, the aeronauts had to throw out everything in the car, and finally to strip themselves of their clothing. On the day after their arrival the two adventurers were splendidly feted at Calais, and Blanchard was presented with the citizenship of the town in a box of gold. The municipal council asked permission to purchase the balloon, and to deposit it in the church, as a memorial of the experiment: the car may still be seen in the Museum of Calais. These honours were not the only ones which Blanchard obtained. A few days after, the fortunate aeronaut received a command to appear before His Majesty the King of France, who awarded him a pension of fifty pounds.

The Queen condescended to stake a sum on his behalf at cards. The courtier, who had the game in his hand, had the good taste to lose a pretty round sum, which was immediately handed over to "Don Quixote de la Mancha," as those who envied his good luck dubbed him.

Illustration of Blanchard's balloon crossing the Channel.

The balloon carrying Blanchard and Jefferies across the English Channel from west to east.

"Le Suffren", piloted by Coustard de Massi and R. P. Mouchet, was designed to traverse the Alps. The illustration above shows it during testing.

THE DEATH OF ROZIER

By William J. Claxton *The Mastery of the Air* (1914)

Not wanting to be overshadowed by Blanchard's successful crossing from England to France, Rozier took up the challenge of attempting to cross in the other direction. The winds were far less favourable and consistent going from east to west, but in the end it was a design failure that proved to be fatal for the great aeronaut and his passenger. On 15th June 1785, Jean-François Pilâtre de Rozier and Pierre Romain became the first recorded fatalities in the history of ballooning.

This daring Frenchman decided to cross the Channel, and to prevent the gas cooling, and the balloon falling into the sea, he hit on the idea of suspending a small fire balloon under the neck of another balloon inflated with hydrogen gas. In the light of our modern knowledge of the highly-inflammable nature of hydrogen, we wonder how anyone could have attempted such an adventure; but there had been little experience of this newly-discovered gas in those days. We are not surprised to read that, when high in the air, there was an awful explosion and the brave aeronaut fell to the earth and was dashed to death.

Although Rozier's voyage led to tragedy, the concept of his hybrid balloon was built upon to produce balloons with a very long flight time. This type of balloon, with separate chambers for a non-heated lifting gas (such as hydrogen or helium) and a heated gas (as used in a Montgolfiere), are known as Rozière balloons in his honour. It was in a Rozière balloon, the Breitling Orbiter 3, that Bertrand Piccard and Brian Jones became the first aeronauts to circumnavigate the earth on 21st March 1999. The flight lasted 477 hours, 47 minutes.

An illustration of the explosion that ended Rozier's attempt to cross the channel.

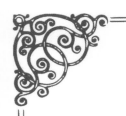

THE LAST OF BLANCHARD

By W. de Fonvielle from *Adventures in the Air* (1877)

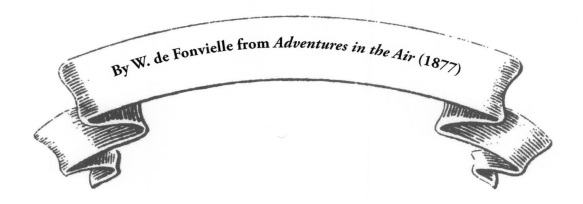

The nature of "balloonomania" at the turn of the 19th century is nicely captured by the following passage. It shows that although ballooning may have been a noble pursuit, it was also a commercial one, and a career for aeronauts like Blanchard. You certainly cannot blame the daring aviators for demanding compensation for their efforts. Ballooning was both an expensive and risky endeavour, as is clearly illustrated by the demise of Blanchard.

The ascent made by Blanchard in company with Lalande was his last triumph. On February 19th, 1800, he made his forty-sixth ascent at Nantes, the citizens of which he rebuked on account of their ungenerous conduct. Groups of close-fisted spectators perched themselves economically on the heights in the neighbourhood of the place of ascent, in order to enjoy the spectacle without payment. Blanchard was naturally irritated at such conduct, and published a thundering manifesto against the economical people of Nantes. "My object," he said, "is not to acquire glory, but to obtain the fruit of my labour. Notwithstanding my love for an aeronautical career, I declare that I shall for the future stick to the solid earth, the public having put it out of my power to make new experiments. I therefore make an end here of my ascents, and my aerial flotilla is for sale. My collection of balloons is composed of 1,800 ells of taffeta of good quality. I shall give good bargains to any amateurs desirous of purchasing. These dismembered balloons will make excellent cloaks, caps, aprons, and umbrellas."

This lament ends by a last appeal to the rich Nantais, of whom he gives a long list, and who had taken up advantageous positions that they might enjoy the ascent gratis. "I beg to inform them," adds the chagrined aeronaut," that they all owe me a contribution equal to the price of the back seats, which is fixed at thirty sous." Blanchard took care to give his address, which was at the house of Citizen Guros, hairdresser, Rue de la Comedie-Brulee. We are glad to believe that this appeal *ad latrones* was listened to, for Blanchard did not sell his stock-in-trade.

We find him at Lyons making his fifty-fifth ascent, troubled by an unexpected event. He found it so cold that when he attempted to open the valve be could not manage it: the lid was soldered to its seat. Luckily, by dint of pulling at the cord, he managed to break the ice, which had compelled him to stray into lofty regions, much against his will.

Here is another curious accident. A violent wind blew at the time of Blanchard's departure on one occasion, at Lyons also. He had remained five hours in the air, and very naturally thought he must have run an immense distance. But, after being buffeted between a multitude of counter currents, the balloon came down quite close to Lyons. For five consecutive hours he bad been the sport of the winds, which made him describe a regular network of zigzags.

The last ascent of this adventurous son of the air was made near the Hague, at the castle of the King' of Holland, early in February 1808. Contrary to his custom, Blanchard made use, on this occasion, of a montgolfiere. Scarcely had he left the ground when he felt himself seized with an attack of apoplexy. He all at once became quite powerless. The fire upon which he had been about to throw some straw, went out. The machine fell heavily to the ground from a height of sixty feet, and the unfortunate man lay stunned like a gymnast who has missed his trapeze. King Louis, who was present when the balloon started, hastened to give his fellow-country-man all the help which his position required. Blanchard recovered consciousness. He was able to be carried to Paris, which he reached sadly enfeebled in mind as well as body. His mental state was so eccentric that the medical journals of the time described and commented upon all the details of his peculiar affection.

Blanchard's finances were in no better condition than his health, for the pension which Louis XVI. had awarded him after he crossed the Channel had been suppressed along with all other Court pensions.

Blanchard died March 7, 1809, without having had any real influence on the progress of aeronautics. He may be blamed for his vanity and a sort of charlatanism, for which there is little excuse; but he deserves to be remembered, not only for the daring with which he faced the perils of an aerial journey across the sea, but for a multitude of attempts, some of which were crowned with success.

THE FIRST BALLOON ASCENT IN ENGLAND

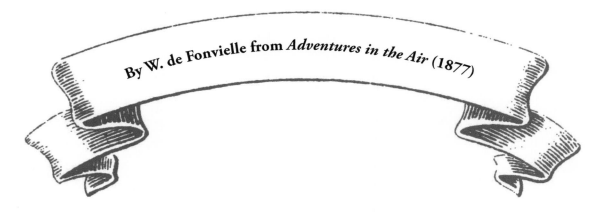

By W. de Fonvielle from *Adventures in the Air* (1877)

Although France ignited the flame of aeronautics, it soon began to travel the continent. Many would-be balloonists heard of the success of the Montgolfiers and started producing their own flying machines. On British shores, the honour of being the first to make a free flight belongs to a little known Scot, James Tytler, but he is often overshadowed by the achievements of the Italian aeronaut, Vincenzo Lunardi, who was the first balloonist to ascend in England. The author of the following piece, a British aeronaut himself, tries to redress the balance and apportion Tytler the credit he deserves, while also documenting the subsequent successes of Lunardi.

As may be supposed, it was not long before the balloon was introduced into England. Indeed, the first successful ascent on record made in our own country took place in the summer of 1784, ten months previous to the fatal venture [Rozier's death]. Now, it is a remarkable and equally regrettable circumstance that though the first ascent on British soil was undoubtedly made by one of our own countrymen, the fact is almost universally forgotten, or ignored, and the credit is accorded to a foreigner.

Let us in strict honesty examine into the case. Vincent Lunardi, an Italian, Secretary to the Neapolitan Ambassador, Prince Caramanico, being in England in the year 1784, determined on organising and personally executing an ascent from London; and his splendid enterprise, which was presently carried to a successful issue, will form the principal subject of the present chapter. It will be seen that remarkable success crowned his efforts, and that his first and ever memorable voyage was carried through on September 15th of that year.

More than a month previously, however, attention had been called to the fact that a Mr. Tytler was preparing to make an ascent from Edinburgh in a hot air balloon, and in the London Chronicle of August 27th occurs the following circumstantial and remarkable letter from a correspondent to that journal:

James Tytler was a Scottish apothecary and the editor of the second edition of Encyclopædia Britannica.

"Edinburgh, Aug. 27, 1784.

"Mr. Tytler has made several improvements upon his fire balloon. The reason of its failure formerly was its being made of porous linen, through which the air made its escape. To remedy this defect, Mr. Tytler has got it covered with a varnish to retain the inflammable air after the balloon is filled.

"Early this morning this bold adventurer took his first aerial flight. The balloon being filled at Comely Garden, he seated himself in the basket, and the ropes being cut he ascended very high and descended quite gradually on the road to Restalrig, about half a mile from the place where he rose, to the great satisfaction of those spectators who were present. Mr. Tytler went up without the furnace this morning; when that is added he will be able to feed the balloon with inflammable air, and continue his aerial excursions as long as he chooses.

"Mr. Tytler is now in high spirits, and in his turn laughs at those infidels who ridiculed his scheme as visionary and impracticable. Mr. Tytler is the first person in Great Britain who has navigated the air."

Referring to this exploit, Tytler, in a laudatory epistle addressed to Lunardi, tells of the difficulties he had had to contend with, and artlessly reveals the cool, confident courage he must have displayed. No shelter being available for the inflation, and a strong wind blowing, his first misfortune was the setting fire to his wicker gallery. The next was the capsizing and damaging of his balloon, which he had lined with paper. He now substituted a coat of varnish for the paper, and his gallery being destroyed, so that he could no longer attempt to take up a stove, he resolved to ascend without one. In the end the balloon was successfully inflated, when he had the hardihood to entrust himself to a small basket (used for carrying earthenware) slung below, and thus to launch himself into the sky. He did so under the conviction that the risk he ran was greater than it really was, for he argued that his craft was now only like a projectile, and "must undoubtedly come to the ground with the same velocity with which it ascended." On this occasion the crowd tried for some time to hold him near the ground by one of the restraining ropes, so that his flight was curtailed. In a second experiment, however, he succeeded in rising some hundreds of feet, and came to earth without mishap.

But little further information respecting Mr. Tytler is apparently forthcoming, and therefore beyond recording the fact that he was the first British aeronaut, and also that he was the first to achieve a balloon ascent in Great Britain, we are unable to make further mention of him in this history.

Of his illustrious contemporary already mentioned there is, on the contrary, much to record, and we would desire to give full credit to his admirable courage and perseverance. It was with

Illustration of James Tytler's fire balloon

a certain national and pardonable pride that the young Italian planned his bold exploit, feeling with a sense of self-satisfaction, which he is at no pains to hide, that he aimed at winning honour for his country as well as for himself. In a letter which he wrote to his guardian, Chevalier Gherardo Compagni, he alludes to the stolid indifference of the English people and philosophers to the brilliant achievements in aeronautics which had been made and so much belauded on the Continent. He proclaims the rivalry as regards science and art existing between France and England, attributing to the latter an attitude of sullen jealousy. At the same time he is fully alive to the necessity of gaining English patronage, and sets about securing this with tactful diplomacy. First he casts about for a suitable spot where his enterprise would not fail to enlist general attention and perhaps powerful patrons, and here he is struck by the attractions and facilities offered by Chelsea Hospital. He therefore applies to Sir George Howard, the Governor, asking for the use of the famous hospital, to which, on the occasion of his experiments, he desires that admittance should only be granted to subscribers, while any profits should be devoted to the pensioners of the hospital. His application having been granted, he assures his guardian that he "still maintains his mental balance, and his sleep is not banished by the magnitude of his enterprise, which is destined to lead him through the path of danger to glory."

This letter was dated the 15th of July, and by the beginning of August his advertisement was already before the public, inviting subscribers and announcing a private view of his balloon at the Lyceum, where it was in course of construction, and was being fitted with contrivances of his own in the shape of oars and sails. He had by this time not only enlisted the interest of Sir George Howard, and of Sir Joseph Banks, but had secured the direct patronage of the King.

But within a fortnight a most unforeseen mishap had occurred, which threatened to overwhelm Lunardi in disappointment and ruin. A Frenchman of the name of Moret, designing to turn to his own advertisement the attention attracted by Lunardi's approaching trials, attempted to forestall the event by an enterprise of his own, announcing that he would make an ascent with a hot air balloon in some gardens near Chelsea Hospital, and at a date previous to that fixed upon by Lunardi. In attempting, however, to carry out this unworthy project the adventurer met with the discomfiture he deserved. He failed to effect his inflation, and when after fruitless attempts continued for three hours, his balloon refused to rise, a large crowd, estimated at 60,000, assembled outside, broke into the enclosure, committing havoc on all sides, not unattended with acts of violence and robbery.

The whole neighbourhood became alarmed, and it followed as a matter of course that Lunardi was peremptorily ordered to discontinue his preparations, and to announce in the public press that his ascent from Chelsea Hospital was forbidden. Failure and ruin now stared the young enthusiast in the face, and it was simply the generous feeling of the British public, and the desire to see fair play, that gave him another chance. As it was, he became the hero of the hour; thousands flocked to the show rooms at the Lyceum, and he shortly obtained fresh grounds, together with needful protection for his project, at the hands of the Hon. Artillery Company. By the 15th of September all incidental difficulties, the mere enumeration of which would unduly swell these pages, had been overcome by sheer persistence, and Lunardi stood in the enclosure allotted him, his preparations in due order, with 150,000 souls, who had formed for hours a dense mass of spectators, watching intently and now confidently the issue of his bold endeavour.

But his anxieties were as yet far from over, for a London crowd had never yet witnessed a balloon ascent, while but a month ago they had seen and wreaked their wrath upon the failure of an adventurer. They were not likely to be more tolerant now. And when the advertised hour for departure had arrived, and the balloon remained inadequately inflated, matters began to take a more serious turn. Half an hour later they approached a crisis, when it began to be known that the balloon still lacked buoyancy, and that the supply of gas was manifestly insufficient. The impatience of the mob indeed was kept in restraint by one man alone. This man was the Prince of Wales who, refusing to join the company within the building and careless of the attitude of the crowd, remained near the balloon to check disorder and unfair treatment.

But an hour after time the balloon still rested inert and then, with fine resolution, Lunardi tried one last expedient. He bade his colleague, Mr. Biggen, who was to have ascended with him, remain behind, and quietly substituting a smaller and lighter wicker car, or rather gallery, took his place within and severed the cords just as the last gun fired. The Prince of Wales raised his hat, imitated at once by all the bystanders, and the first balloon that ever quitted English soil rose into the air amid the extravagant enthusiasm of the multitude. The intrepid aeronaut, pardonably excited, and fearful lest he should not be seen within the gallery, made frantic efforts to attract attention by waving his flag, and worked his oars so vigorously that one of them broke and fell. A pigeon also gained its freedom and escaped. The voyager, however, still retained companions in his venture—a dog and a cat.

Following his own account, Lunardi's first act on finding himself fairly above the town was to fortify himself with some glasses of wine, and to devour the leg of a chicken. He describes the city as a vast beehive, St. Paul's and other churches standing out prominently; the streets shrunk to lines, and all humanity apparently transfixed and watching him. A little later he is equally struck with the view of the open country, and his ecstasy is pardonable in a novice. The verdant pastures eclipsed the visions of his own lands. The precision of boundaries impressed him with a sense of law and order, and of good administration in the country where he was a sojourner.

By this time he found his balloon, which had been only two-thirds full at starting, to be so distended that he was obliged to untie the mouth to release the strain. He also found that the condensed moisture round the neck had frozen. These two statements point to his having reached a considerable altitude, which is intelligible enough. It is, however, difficult to believe his further assertion that by the use of his single oar he succeeded in working himself down to within a few hundred feet of the earth. The descent of the balloon must, in point of fact, have been due to a copious outrush of gas at his former altitude. Had his oar really been effective in working the balloon down it would not have needed the discharge of ballast presently spoken of to cause it to reascend. Anyhow, he found himself sufficiently near the earth to land a passenger who was anxious to get out. His cat had not been comfortable in the cold upper regions, and now at its urgent appeal was deposited in a corn field, which was the point of first contact with the earth. It was carefully received by a country-woman, who promptly sold it to a gentleman on the other side of the hedge, who had been pursuing the balloon.

The first ascent of a balloon in England was deserving of some record, and an account alike circumstantial and picturesque is forthcoming. The novel and astonishing sight was witnessed by a Hertfordshire farmer, whose testimony, published by Lunardi in the same year, runs as follows:—

This deponent on his oath sayeth that, being on Wednesday, the 15th day of September instant, between the hours of three and four in the afternoon, in a certain field called Etna, in the parish of North Mimms aforesaid, he perceived a large machine sailing in the air, near the place where he was on horseback; that the machine continuing to approach the earth, the part of it in which this deponent perceived a gentleman standing came to the ground and dragged a short way on the ground in a slanting direction; that the time when this machine thus touched the earth was, as near as this deponent could judge, about a quarter before four in the afternoon. That this deponent being on horseback, and his horse restive, he could not approach nearer to the machine than about four poles, but that he could plainly perceive therein gentleman dressed in light coloured cloaths, holding in his hand a trumpet, which had the appearance of silver or bright tin. That by this time several harvest men coming up from the other part of the field, to the number of twelve men and thirteen women, this deponent called to them to endeavour to stop the machine, which the men attempted, but the gentleman in the machine desiring them to desist, and the machine moving with considerable rapidity, and clearing the earth, went off in a north direction and continued in sight at a very great height for near an hour afterwards. And this deponent further saith that the part of the machine in the which the gentleman stood did not actually touch the ground for more than half

Mr. Lunardi's New Balloon, 13th May 1785.

Exhibition of Lunardi's balloon at the Pantheon in Oxford Street, London.

a minute, during which time the gentleman threw out a parcel of what appeared to this deponent as dry sand. That after the machine had ascended again from the earth this deponent perceived a grapple with four hooks, which hung from the bottom of the machine, dragging along the ground, which carried up with it into the air a small parcel of loose oats, which the women were raking in the field. And this deponent further on his oath sayeth that when the machine had risen clear from the ground about twenty yards the gentleman spoke to this deponent and to the rest of the people with his trumpet, wishing them goodbye and saying that he should soon go out of sight. And this deponent further on his oath sayeth that the machine in which the gentleman came down to earth appeared to consist of two distinct parts connected together by ropes, namely that in which the gentleman appeared to be, a stage boarded at the bottom, and covered with netting and ropes on the sides about four feet and a half high, and the other part of the machine appeared in the shape of an urn, about thirty feet high and of about the same diameter, made of canvas like oil skin, with green, red, and yellow stripes.

NATHANIEL WHITBREAD.

Sworn before me this twentieth day of September, 1784, WILLIAM BAKER.

It was a curious fact, pointed out to the brave Italian by a resident, that the field in which the temporary descent had been made was called indifferently Etna or Italy, "from the circumstance which attended the late enclosure of a large quantity of roots, rubbish, etc., having been collected there, and having continued burning for many days. The common people having heard of a burning mountain in Italy gave the field that name."

But the voyage did not end at Etna. The, as yet, inexperienced aeronaut now cast out all available ballast in the shape of sand, as also his provisions, and rising with great speed, soon reached a greater altitude than before, which he sought to still farther increase by throwing down his plates, knives, and forks. In this somewhat reckless expenditure he thought himself justified by the reliance he placed on his oar, and it is not surprising that in the end he owns that he owed his safety in his final descent to his good fortune. The narrative condensed concludes thus:—

"At twenty minutes past four I descended in a meadow near Ware. Some labourers were at work in it. I requested their assistance, but they exclaimed they would have nothing to do with one who came on the Devil's Horse, and no entreaties could prevail on them to approach me. I at last owed my deliverance to a young woman in the field who took hold of a cord I had thrown out, and, calling to the men, they yielded that assistance at her request which they had refused to mine."

As may be supposed, Lunardi's return to London resembled a royal progress. Indeed, he was welcomed as a conqueror to whom the whole town sought to do honour, and perhaps his greatest gratification came by way of the accounts he gathered of incidents which occurred during his eventful voyage. At a dinner at which he was being entertained by the Lord Mayor and judges he learned that a lady seeing his falling oar, and fancying that he himself was dashed to pieces, received a shock thereby which caused her death. Commenting on this, one of the judges bade him be reassured, inasmuch as he had, as if by compensation, saved the life of a young man who might live to be reformed. The young man was a criminal whose condemnation was regarded as certain at the hands of the jury before whom he was being arraigned, when tidings reached the court that Lunardi's balloon was in the air. On this so much confusion arose that the jury were unable to give due deliberation to the case, and, fearing to miss the great sight, actually agreed to acquit the prisoner, that they themselves might be free to leave the court!

But he was flattered by a compliment of a yet higher order. He was told that while he hovered over London the King was in conference with his principal Ministers, and his Majesty, learning that he was in the sky, is reported to have said to his councillors, "We may resume our own deliberations at pleasure, but we may never see poor Lunardi again!" On this, it is further stated that the conference broke up, and the King, attended by Mr. Pitt and other chief officers of State, continued to view Lunardi through telescopes as long as he remained in the horizon.

The public Press, notably the Morning Post of September 16, paid a worthy tribute to the hero of the hour, and one last act of an exceptional character was carried out in his honour, and remains in evidence to this hour. In a meadow in the parish of Standon, near Ware, there stands a rough hewn stone, now protected by an iron rail. It marks the spot where Lunardi landed, and on it is cut a legend which runs thus:

Let Posterity know
And knowing be astonished that
On the 15th day of September 1784
Vincent Lunardi of Lusca in Tuscany
The first aerial traveller in Britain
Mounting from the Artillery Ground
In London
And Traversing the Regions of the Air
For Two Hours and Fifteen Minutes
In this Spot Revisited the Earth.
On this rude monument
For ages be recorded
That Wondrous Enterprise
Successfully atchieved
By the Powers of Chemistry
And the Fortitude of Man
That Improvement in Science
Which
The Great Author of all Knowledge
Patronyzing by His Providence
The Invention of Mankind
Hath graciously permitted
To Their Benefit
And
His own Eternal Glory.

Captain Vincenzo Lunardi with his assistant George Biggin, and Mrs. Letitia Anne Sage, in a balloon (John Francis Rigaud, 1785).

This print shows Lunardi making the first balloon ascent in Spain in 1792.

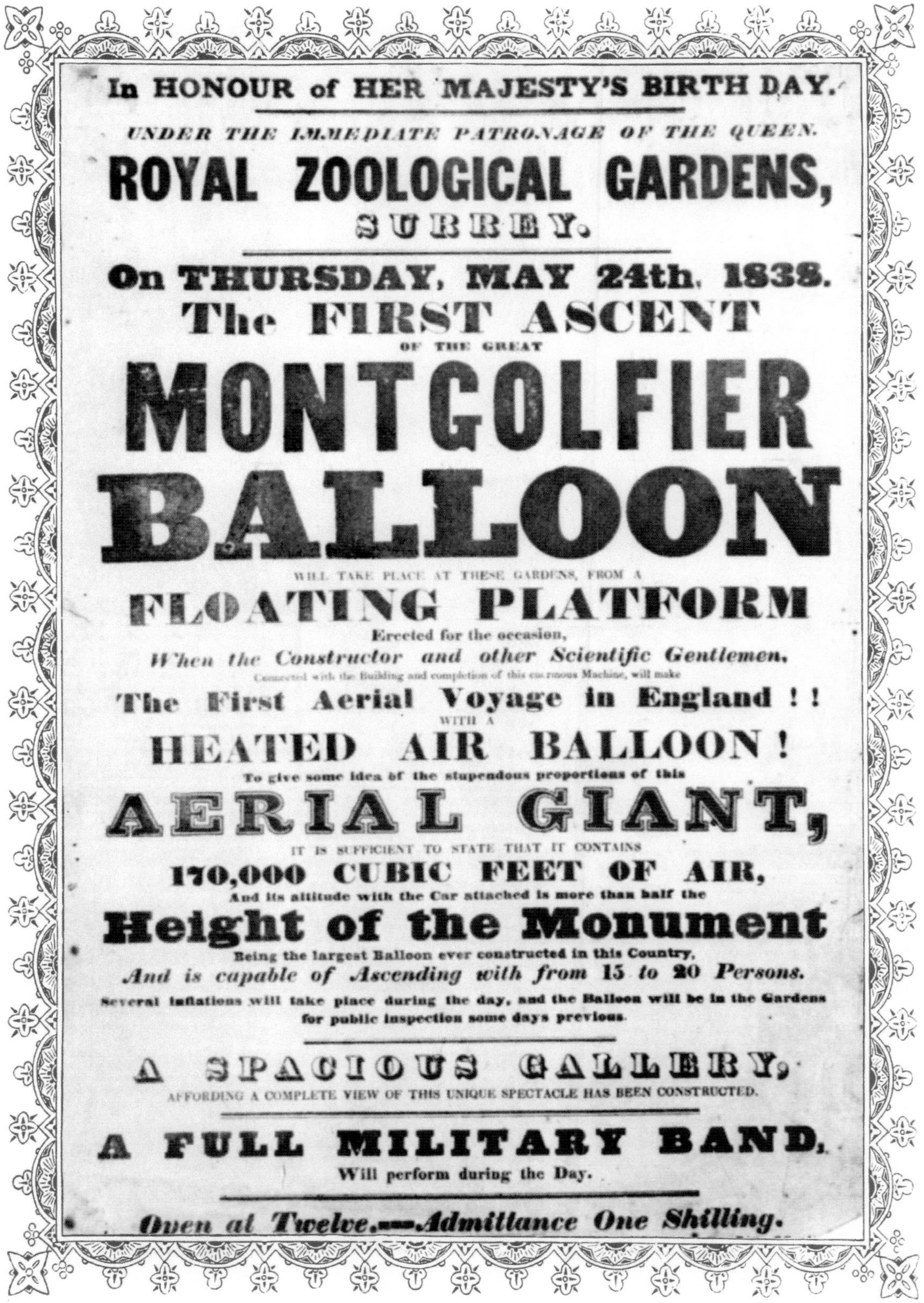

An advert for the ascent of a huge balloon in England.

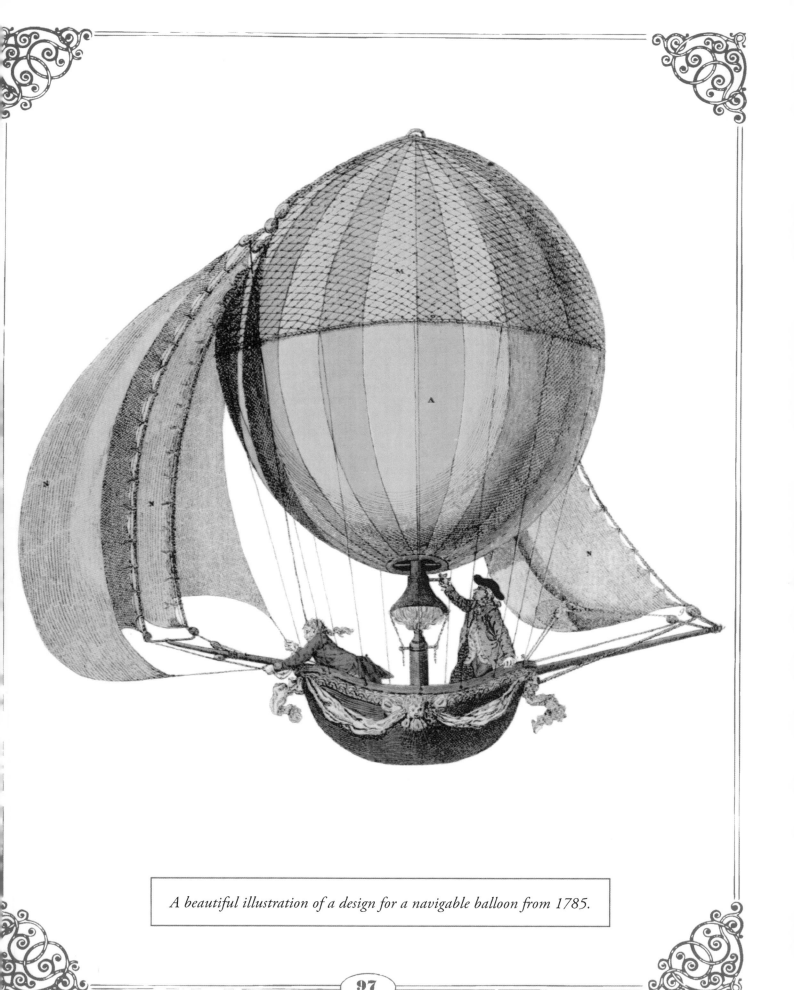

A beautiful illustration of a design for a navigable balloon from 1785.

JAMES SADLER

James Sadler was the second person, following Vincenzo Lunardi, to make a balloon ascent in England on 4th October 1784, a feat which also made him the first English aeronaut. He made a subsequent attempt to cross the Channel but unfortunately descended in the Thames Estuary.

As well as being a national celebrity for his ballooning exploits, he was also a accomplished scientist, making several patented steam engine designs, and improving cannon design. Sadler's adjustments to the smelting process optimised the efficiency and accuracy of cannons, an achievement he was praised for by Lord Nelson. Even though incredibly famous in his own time, he is little remembered in the history books. This might be because he has been overshadowed by his European counterparts, or maybe because his humble origins as a pastry chef didn't endear him to the academics and aristocracy of his time. Whatever the reason, conducting 50 flights over 40 years and creating numerous innovations, James Sadler's name belongs among those of the great pioneers of aerostation.

Sadler's balloon at the jubilee celebration of 1814. Sadler's son John ascended in the balloon and dropped out jubilee messages attached to parachutes. Engraving by John Pitts.

Ascent of Mr. Sadler the celebrated British aeronaut at Nottingham, 1st November 1813.

This satirical print by William Elmes depicts one of James Sadler's early balloon ascents in England. The scene is of the celebrations of the Regent's birthday.

This satirical cartoon by James Gillray ridicules Lord Grenville's installation as the Chancellor of Oxford University in 1810.

'The Minerva Balloon'
The ambitious design in by Étienne-Gaspard Robert (aka Professor Robertson) (1763-1837).

'The Minerva Balloon'

Étienne-Gaspard Robert (aka Professor Robertson) (1763-1837), a Belgian stage magician, phantasmagoria pioneer, and aeronaut, produced this ambitious design in the early 19th century. He was extremely optimistic about the future of ballooning – this craft being 80 tonnes and intended to carry 60 passengers for several months at a time. He obviously received some less than positive reviews for his design, but remained confident in its realisation. Here is what he had to say about his invention:

"Thus this invention, after having at first electrified all savants from the one end of the world to the other, has suffered the fate of all discoveries—it was all at once arrested. Did not astronomy wait long for Newton, and chemistry for Lavoisier, to raise them to something like the splendour they now enjoy? Was not the magnet a long time a toy in the hands of the Chinese, without giving birth to the idea of the compass? The electric fluid was known in the time of Thales, but how many ages did we wait for the discovery of galvanism? Yet these sciences, which may be studied in silent retreats, were more likely to yield fruit to the discoverer than aerostatics, which demand courage and skill, and of which the experiments, which are always public, are attended with great cost."

COUNT ZAMBECCARI AND HIS PERILOUS TRIP ACROSS THE ADRIATIC

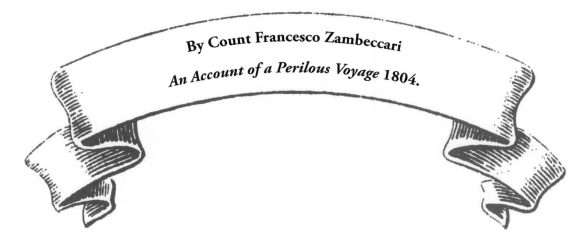

By Count Francesco Zambeccari

An Account of a Perilous Voyage 1804.

Count Francesco Zambeccari was an Italian balloonist and the first person to launch an unmanned balloon in England, in 1783. Zambeccari, despite his best efforts, was an ill-fated aeronaut. During his ballooning career he set himself on fire, crashed into the Adriatic Sea twice, and eventually died when his balloon caught fire and crash landed in 1812. The following is his harrowing account of a perilous voyage in 1804.

It was two o'clock. The compass had been broken, and was useless; the wax light in the lantern would not burn in such a rarefied atmosphere. We descended gently across a thick layer of whitish clouds, and when we had got below them, Andreoli heard a sound, muffled and almost inaudible, which he immediately recognised as the breaking of waves in the distance. Instantly he announced to me this new and fearful danger. I listened, and had not long to wait before I was convinced that he was speaking the truth. It was necessary to have light to examine the state of the barometer, and thus ascertain what was our elevation above the sea level, and to take our measures in consequence. Andreoli broke five phosphoric matches, without getting a spark of fire. Nevertheless, we succeeded, after very great difficulty, by the help of the flint and steel, in lighting the lantern. It was now three o'clock in the morning—we had started at midnight. The sound of the waves, tossing with wild uproar, became louder and louder, and I suddenly saw the surface of the sea violently agitated just below us. I immediately seized a large sack of sand, but had not time to throw it over before we were all in the water, gallery and all. In the first moment of fright, we threw into the sea everything that would lighten the balloon—our ballast, all our instruments, a portion of our clothing, our money,

Count Zambeccari and his passengers trying to attract the attention of a passing ship.

and the oars. As, in spite of all this, the balloon did not rise, we threw over our lamp also. After having torn and cut away everything that did not appear to us to be of indispensable necessity, the balloon, thus very much lightened, rose all at once, but with such rapidity and to such a prodigious elevation, that we had difficulty in hearing each other, even when shouting at the top of our voices. I was ill, and vomited severely. Grassetti was bleeding at the nose; we were both breathing short and hard, and felt oppression on the chest. As we were thrown upon our backs at the moment when the balloon took such a sudden start out of the water and bore us with such swiftness to those high regions, the cold seized us suddenly, and we found ourselves covered all at once with a coating of ice. I could not account for the reason why the moon, which was in its last quarter, appeared on a parallel line with us, and looked red as blood.

"After having traversed these regions for half an hour, at an immeasurable elevation, the balloon slowly began to descend, and at last we fell again into the sea, at about four in the morning I cannot determine at what distance we were from land when we fell the second time. The night was very dark, the sea rolling heavily, and we were in no condition to make observations. But it must have been in the middle of the Adriatic that we fell. Although we descended gently, the gallery was sunk, and we were often entirely covered with water. The balloon being now more than half empty, in consequence of the vicissitudes through, which we had passed, gave a purchase to the wind, which pressed against it as against a sail, so that by means of it we were dragged and beaten about at the mercy of the storm and the waves. At daybreak we looked out and found ourselves opposite Pesaro, four miles from the shore. We were comforting ourselves with the prospect of a safe landing, when a wind from the land drove us with violence away over the open sea. It was now full day, but all we could see were the sea, the sky, and the death that threatened us. Certainly some boats happened to come within sight; but no sooner did they see the balloon floating and striping upon the water than they made all sail to get away from it. No hope was then left to us but the very small one of making the coasts of Dalmatia, which were opposite, but at a great distance from us. Without the slightest doubt we should have been drowned if heaven had not mercifully directed towards us a navigator who, better informed than those we had seen before, recognised our machine to be a balloon and quickly sent his long-boat to our rescue. The sailors threw us a stout cable, which we attached to the gallery, and by means of which they rescued us when fainting with exposure. The balloon thus lightened, immediately rose into the air, in spite of all the efforts of the sailors who wished to capture it. The long boat received a severe shock from its escape, as the rope was still attached to it, and the sailors hastened to cut themselves free. At once the balloon mounted with incredible rapidity, and was lost in the clouds, where it disappeared for ever from our view. It was eight in the morning when we got on board. Grassetti was so ill that he hardly showed any signs of life. His hands were sadly mutilated. Cold, hunger, and the dreadful anxiety had completely prostrated me. The brave captain of the vessel did everything in his power to restore us. He conducted us safely to Ferrara, whence we were carried to Pola, where we were received with the greatest kindness, and where I was compelled to have my fingers amputated.

The best way of travel, however, if you aren't in any hurry at all, if you don't care where you are going, if you don't like to use your legs, if you don't want to be annoyed at all by any choice of directions, is in a balloon. In a balloon, you can decide only when to start, and usually when to stop. The rest is left entirely to nature.

– William Pene du Bois,
The Twenty-one Balloons.
published in 1947 by the
Viking Press

PARACHUTES

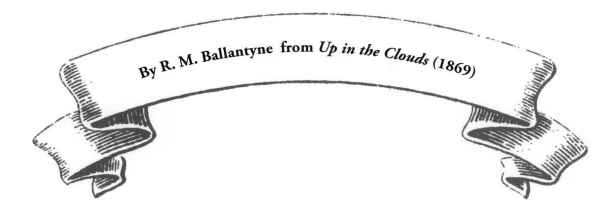

By R. M. Ballantyne from *Up in the Clouds* (1869)

There was an obvious need for the development of some sort of safety device to combat the all too apparent dangers the aeronauts faced. This came in the form of the parachute, saving its first life in 1793 when Pierre Blanchard had to escape from a ruptured balloon. He survived but did break his leg upon landing. The first successful jump was made four years later by Andre Jacques Garnerin who proved its use as an essential element in the balloonist's toolkit. Of course many people now enjoy the use of parachutes for sport and pleasure, and the technology is now well understood and generally safe. 200 years ago however, it was a considerable leap of faith, and just like ballooning itself, this burgeoning technology also claimed its victims.

This contrivance has been considered by some a very important adjunct to the balloon; whether it be so or no, we do not pretend to determine, but certainly it is an interesting and curious machine, which merits notice.

The parachute may be described as a species of gigantic umbrella attached to the balloon below the car, which hangs in a loose form while ascending, but expands, of necessity, when cut adrift and allowed to descend. As the balloon has a car hung beneath it, so in like manner the parachute has a small car or basket, capable of holding one person, suspended from it. The word signifies a *guard against falling*—from the French *parer*, to ward off, and *chute*, a fall, and is allied to *parasol*, which means literally "a warder off of the sun."

The parachute was introduced some years after a terrible accident which occurred to the celebrated aeronaut Rozier, who, desirous of emulating Blanchard and Jeffries by crossing the channel from France to England in a balloon, made an attempt, which cost him his life. Rozier's balloon was about forty feet in diameter, and had attached to it, beneath, a smaller balloon on the Montgolfier principle. On the 15th of June 1785, he entered the car with Monsieur Romain, and ascended to the height of above three thousand feet, when it was observed by the spectators that the lower balloon had caught fire. With horror they saw that the fire spread—the whole apparatus was in a blaze—and in another minute it descended like a shattered meteor to the ground with a terrible crash. It fell near the sea-shore, about four miles from Boulogne, and of course the unfortunate voyagers were killed instantaneously. At a later period a Venetian nobleman and his lady fell with their balloon from a great height and were killed. It must be remarked, however, that cases of this kind were very rare, considering the rage which there was at that period for ballooning.

In order to provide aeronauts with a means of escape—a last resource in case of accident—the parachute was invented. It may be regarded as a balloon's lifeboat, which will (perhaps!) bear the passengers in safety to the ground in case of balloon-wreck.

Doubtless the umbrella suggested the parachute. Every one knows the tremendous force that this implement exerts in a high wind if the unfortunate owner should happen to get turned round in the wrong direction. The men of the east have, it is said, turned this power to account by making use of an umbrella to enable them to leap from considerable heights. In particular, a native of Siam, who was noted for his feats of agility, was wont to amuse the King and his court by taking tremendous leaps, having two small umbrellas with long slender handles attached to his girdle. These eased him down in safety, but he was occasionally driven by the wind against trees or houses, and sometimes into a neighbouring river.

In case any adventurous individual should be tempted to make trial of the powers of himself and his umbrella in this way, we think it right, by way of caution, to tell him that the French General Bournonville, who was imprisoned in

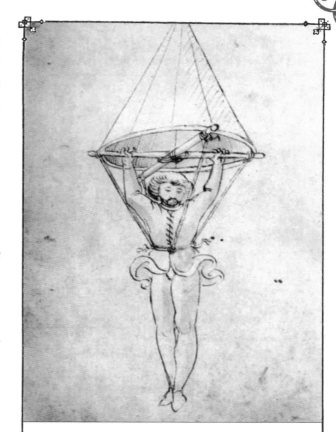

This is the oldest known illustration of a parachute, by an unknown artist from Italy in the 1470s.

An advert for a demonstration of Garnerin's parachute.

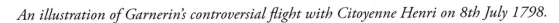
An illustration of Garnerin's controversial flight with Citoyenne Henri on 8th July 1798.

Garnerin was a French aeronaut and student of ballooning pioneer, professor Jacques Charles. He regularly conducted tests and demonstrations of his aeronautical developments at Parc Monceau, Paris, and in 1797 he caused quite a stir when he announced his next flight to depart from the park would include a female passenger; Citoyenne Henri. This resulted in Garnerin being forced to appear before officials at the Central Bureau of Police to justify his project. They were particularly concerned with the effects of altitude on the delicate female body but also with the moral implications of an unmarried man and woman being in such close proximity to one another. The police issued an injunction to stop Garnerin from proceeding, but it was later overturned and the pair made their ascent in front of a large crowd of spectators. The voyage was a successful one, travelling about 30 kilometres before landing in Goussainville.

the fortress of Olmutz in 1793, became so desperate that he attempted to regain his freedom by leaping with an umbrella from his window, which was forty feet from the ground. He hoped that the umbrella would break his fall. Doubtless it did so to some extent, and saved him from being killed, but being a large heavy man, he came down with sufficient violence to break his leg, and was carried back to his dungeon.

The chief differences between a parachute and an umbrella lie in the great size of the former, and in the cords which stretch from the outer points of its ribs to the lower end of the handle. These cords give it strength, and prevent it from turning inside out. There is also a hole in the top of the parachute to allow some of the air to escape.

The first parachute was constructed by Blanchard in 1785, and a dog was the first living creature that descended in it, and reached the earth unhurt. Blanchard afterwards made a descent in person at Basle, and broke his leg in the fall.

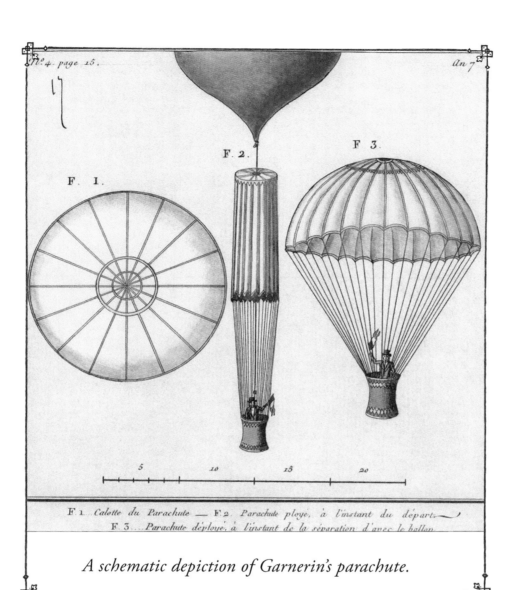

A schematic depiction of Garnerin's parachute.

The bold aeronaut Monsieur Garnerin next ventured to make the perilous descent. He visited London in 1802, and made several ascents in a balloon. During one of these, on the evening of the 2nd November, he cut himself adrift in his parachute when at a vast height. The parachute was made of white canvas, having thirty-two gores, which, when not in use, hung with its cords from a hoop near the top of the machine. When expanded, it formed a vast umbrella of twenty-three feet in diameter, with a small basket about four feet high, and two and a quarter wide, suspended below it. Monsieur Garnerin stood in this basket when his balloon mounted into the air from an enclosure near North Audley Street. The parachute hung like a curtain over his head, above it towered the balloon, beneath stood the anxious multitude.

Well might they gaze in breathless expectation! After floating for some time in the upper regions of the air, as if he dreaded to make the bold attempt, he cut the cord that fastened him to the balloon when at the height, probably, of about half a mile. At first the parachute remained closed and descended with frightful violence; then it burst open, and for some seconds tossed about to such an extent that the basket was sometimes thrown almost into a horizontal position. The wind carried it over Marylebone and Somerstown; it almost grazed some of the houses of Saint Pancras in passing, and finally came to the ground in a field with such violence that poor Garnerin was thrown on his face and severely cut and bruised. No wonder that we are told he received a terrible shock. He trembled violently, and blood flowed from his nose and ears. Nevertheless, the accident did not deter his daughter from afterwards making the descent several times—and in safety.

The cause of the irregularity and violence of Garnerin's descent was the giving way of one of the stays, which had the effect of deranging the balance of the apparatus.

In 1837 Mr Cocking invented a new parachute, which he hoped would be free from the faults of the other. It may be described as being the reverse of that of Garnerin, being made in the form of an

Robert Cocking's unsuccessful parachute demonstration.
Cocking was the first person to be killed in a parachuting accident.

umbrella blown inside out. The resistance to the air, it was thought, would be sufficient to check the rapid descent, while its form would prevent the tendency to oscillate.

This parachute was 34 feet in diameter, and was distended by a strong hoop to prevent its closing. There was also a hole in the middle of it, about 6 feet in diameter. Mr Cocking started from Vauxhall Gardens on the 24th of July, and after ascending to a considerable height, cut himself loose from his balloon when over Blackheath. The parachute descended rapidly and vibrated with great violence; the large hoop broke, the machine collapsed, and the unfortunate aeronaut was killed, and his body dreadfully mutilated.

Fatal accidents of this kind were to be expected; nevertheless it is a fact that the disasters which have befallen aeronauts have been comparatively few, considering the extreme danger to which they are necessarily exposed, not only from the delicacy of the materials with which they operate and the uncertainty of the medium through which they move, but, particularly, because of the impossibility of giving direction to their air-ships, or to arrest their progress through space. Parachutes, however, are not so absolutely incapable of being directed as are balloons. Monsieur Nadar writes on this point as follows:—

"Let us consider the action of the parachute.

"A parachute is a sort of umbrella, in which the handle is replaced at its point of insertion by an opening intended to ease the excess of air, in order to avoid the strong oscillations, chiefly at the moment at which it is first expanded. Cords, departing symmetrically from divers points of the circumference, meet concentrically at the basket in which is the aeronaut. Above this basket, and at the entrance of the folded parachute, that is to say closed during the rise, a hoop of sufficient diameter is intended to facilitate, at the moment of the fall, the entrance of the air which, rushing in under the pressure, expands the folds more easily and rapidly.

"Now the parachute, where the weight of the car, of the attaching cords, and the wrigglings of the aeronaut, is in equilibrium with the expansion—the parachute, which seems to have

An advert for a lecture on the parachute.

Dolly Shepherd in her jump outfit.

no other aim but to moderate the shock in falling—the parachute even has been found capable of being directed, and aeronauts who have practised it, take care not to forget it. If the current is about to drive the aeronaut over a place where the descent is dangerous—say a river, a town, or a forest—the aeronaut perceiving to his right, let us suppose, a piece of ground suitable for his purpose, pulls at the cords which surround the right side, and by thus imparting a greater obliquity to his roof of silk, glides through the air, which it cleaves obliquely, towards the desired spot. Every descent, in fact, is determined by the side on which the incline is greatest."

That these are not mere theoretical opinions or conjectures is certain from the fact that Mademoiselle Garnerin once wagered to guide herself with a parachute from the point of separation from her balloon to a place determined and very remote. By the combined inclinations which could be given to her parachute, she was seen in fact, very distinctly, to manoeuvre and tend towards the appointed place, and succeeded at length in alighting within a few yards of it.

Dolly Shepherd.

Since the demonstrations of Garnerin, parachutes have been used to entertain the public. Dolly Shepherd (1887-1983) is a notable example of this breed of daredevils. Her act involved ascending on a trapeze slung below a hot-air balloon, to a height of two to four-thousand feet, before descending on a parachute. On one occasion, Dolly took to the air accompanied by another girl. The intention was that each of them would use their own parachute to descend, but unfortunately, her co-aeronaut's parachute didn't open and she was forced to cling on to Dolly. With both of them sharing a single canopy, the descent was obviously much too fast and the crash landing resulted in Dolly being paralysed for several weeks. However, it was not long before she was back in the air again. Even in her twilight years, Dolly had not lost her appetite for aviation, flying with the Red Devils display team at the age of 96.

FEMALE AERONAUTS

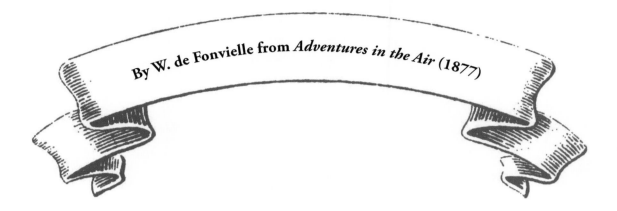

By W. de Fonvielle from *Adventures in the Air* (1877)

Early on in the history of aeronautics, women were taking part in the ascents, but they were generally there for novelty and to add to the romanticism of the voyages. It was not until Sophie Blanchard, wife of Pierre Blanchard, that there was a woman who could command a crowd piloting her own craft. She had at first, been wary of ascending with her husband, but once she did, became bitten by the bug of ballooning, making her first solo ascent in 1805, and continuing to support herself with a career as a balloonist after the death of her husband. Sadly, she too lost her life to the pursuit.

Aeronautics fell quite under female sway during the period between 1810 and 1830. In fact, ascents by women were so brilliant and so numerous that one might have been led to conclude that the male sex had been banished from the sky.

Although Madame Thible, the Sisters Simonnet, Mrs. Sage, and Mlle. Celestine Fleury had preceded Madame Blanchard, the latter must be regarded as the first of female aeronauts; for before her no daughter of Eve had made the aeronautical art a regular profession. A somewhat romantic story is told of the birth and espousal of Madame Blanchard, but we need not repeat it here. It was ten years after her marriage before she could make up her mind to accompany her husband into the air.

Élisabeth Thible was a French opera singer and the first woman on record to ascend in a hot air balloon. On the 4th of June 1784, Thible took her place alongside Mr. Fleurant on 'The Gustave', and dressed as the Roman goddess Minerva, sang two duets from Monsigny's La Belle Arsène – a celebrated opera of the time. The balloon was named in honour of Gustave III of Sweden who was visiting Lyon and present at the ascent. Fleurent credited the success of the flight to Thible's courage in feeding the fire box during the voyage.

In 1805 Madame Blanchard made her first ascent alone. As she was very short and very slender, the balloon which she constructed for her personal use was of very small dimensions. Her car was so light and fragile as to make one giddy to look at it; it had been called a child's cradle. The car of Venus might have been more graceful, but it was not more aerial. These circumstances added to the attractions of the experiment and diminished the expense. Although Madame Blanchard used pure gas for inflating her balloon, she never spent more than 40z. for each experiment. Thus she soon was able to accumulate a little fortune.

She liked to make ascents at nightfall, a time when the winds are supposed by aeronauts to be quietest and when the public could assemble at their ease. She acquired such intrepidity that she only descended when day had appeared. She preferred to sleep in the car, where she was sure no one could come to disturb her. She dreaded descending in unknown places where the least noise would make her tremble like a leaf; for this truly astonishing woman was strangely timid on the earth.

The great aeronaut Sophie Blanchard.

She dreaded riding in a carriage, fearing that every instant it would be overturned. If railways had existed in her day, she would probably have never consented to make use of them.

When Garnerin fell into disgrace, Madame Blanchard became the favourite aeronautical performer at public fêtes; for, in spite of imperial antipathies, balloons had become a necessary accompaniment to every public celebration. On June 24, 1810, on the occasion of the marriage of the Emperor Napoleon with the Grand Duchess Maria Louisa, the Guard held a fête in honour of their sovereign. Napoleon took his place, along with his wife, on the balcony of the Military School, and followed the ascent of Madame Blanchard with the greatest interest.

Madame Blanchard was not the only queen of the air; she had dangerous rivals in the women of the Garnerin family. Eliza, daughter of the elder Garnerin, was a beautiful woman, whose appearance presented a complete contrast to that of her rival, to whom nature had given the complexion of a bird. She visited foreign countries, and especially Spain, where she had a bone to pick with the Corregidor. One of her ascents having failed, Ferdinand VII., who was never ready to listen to reason, caused both father and daughter to be thrown into prison.

Eliza, on her return to France, wrote or signed a violent pamphlet in which she protested with indignation against the treatment to which she had been subjected. Ferdinand VII. could not remain under so grave a charge, and caused one of his retainers of the pen to write a reply not less lively. The de-fender of the King of Spain maintained that Eliza could not start because the father did not know how to prepare pure hydrogen gas by the decomposition of water; that he had calumniated the authorities of Madrid by pretending that they were opposed to her experiment; that his Catholic Majesty had put father and daughter in prison in order to protect them against the fury of the people, and also to compel them to return a portion of their fee.

Madame Blanchard was apt to reckon too much on her good luck and presence of mind. Having once allowed her balloon to go too high, she had almost been frozen to death in a cloud of crystals so fine and so tenacious that they stuck to her face. On another occasion, in the course of 1818, she opened the valve without thinking of what might be the nature of the ground below, and having fallen on the top of some large trees, she remained perched there until some peasants came to her assistance.

Although she never attempted to descend in a parachute, Madame Blanchard, to her misfortune, was tempted to follow the example of the Garnerins, and often illuminated her balloon, sometimes with coloured glasses, sometimes with fireworks. On July 7, 1819, there was a crowd at the Tivoli Gardens. A bombshell gave the signal for ascent. The trees were suddenly illuminated by Bengal lights. Madame Blanchard ascended to the sound of brilliant music. The balloon drew after it an immense star which had been lighted. Faggots like those which were burning in the garden were lit, and the balloon illuminated by mysterious fires glided across the sky like a passing meteor.

Soon there falls a shower of gold which: seems to come from the car. Frantic applause from below reaches the ear of Madame Blanchard. The brave aeronaut is seen to stoop; she lights with a port-fire a bomb of silver rain, which being suspended to a parachute, descends with supernatural majesty.

Unfortunately the balloon, which always continued to ascend, allowed quantities of gas to escape. An unseen jet is lit by the stick. A train of fire shoots out; the balloon is in flames. An enormous jet issues from it. From all parts below the plaudits are redoubled.

But Madame Blanchard is far from sharing the enthusiasm of the ignorant crowd. With a coolness which few men have ever shown in a balloon, she tries to put out the fire. Not succeeding in this, she throws out all her ballast in order to moderate her descent. The unfortunate woman is seen looking down through space, trying to discover towards what point pitiless gravity is about to precipitate her.

Thanks to her presence of mind she will be saved, for the gas, driven back by the sudden increase of pressure, soon re-enters the interior of the balloon and extinguishes itself. There was then in the suburbs near where the balloon was, large gardens where an aeronaut might descend without danger. But the wind drives her on to the roof of a house against which her frail aerial bark strikes, and is over- turned. At the moment of the shock, which is not violent, Madame Blanchard is heard to cry "A moi!" ("Help ! ") But the last hour of the unfortunate daughter of the air has come. In gliding over the roof, her car encounters an iron cramp and is overturned. She does not expect so sudden a shock, and therefore has not been holding on. When the people come up, the car and the balloon are still suspended on the roof, but Madame Blanchard, stretched on the pavement below, with broken shoulder and broken head, is breathing her last.

The body is carried to the Tivoli Gardens. Immediately the music, the dancing, the singing, the illuminations are stopped; a sudden fear seizes the servants; some take to flight.

The tragic death of Sophie Blanchard.

A subscription on the spot realised a good round sum. It was not, however, continued, as it was learned that Madame Blanchard had left a small fortune to the daughter of a friend. The funds collected were employed in raising a graceful tomb at Père La Chaise, instead of being returned to the subscribers, most of them anonymous.

A BALLOON DUEL

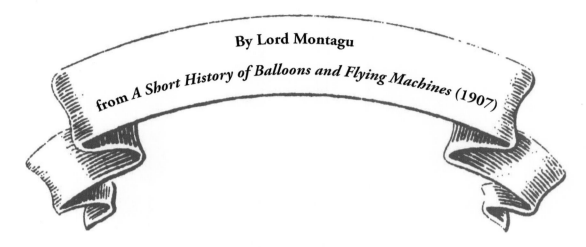

By Lord Montagu

from *A Short History of Balloons and Flying Machines* (1907)

Thankfully, the methods of settling interpersonal quarrels have moved on from the early 19th century and the thought of conducting a duel, to settle a love triangle, seems bizarre even if the duellists were not in balloons. Not only were the protagonists misguided, it must also be noted that they managed to find what must be the most committed 'seconds' in the history of duelling. The following article by Lord Montagu describes the comedy and tragedy of the situation.

Perhaps the most remarkable duel ever fought took place in 1808. M. de Grandprè with M. le Pique, had a quarrel arising out of jealousy concerning a lady engaged at the Imperial Opera.

They agreed to fight a duel to settle their respective claims, and in order that the heat of angry passion should not interfere with the polished elegance of the proceedings they postponed the duel for a month, the lady agreeing to bestow her smiles on the survivor of the two, if the other was killed.

The duellists were to fight in the air, and two balloons were constructed exactly alike. On the day fixed De Grandprè and his second entered the car of one balloon, Le Pique and his second that of the other, it was in the garden of the Tuileries, amid an immense concourse of spectators. The gentlemen were to fire not at each other, but at each other's balloons in order to bring them down by the escape of gas, and each took a blunderbus in his car.

The ropes were cut, the balloons ascended, and about half a mile above the surface of the earth, a preconcerted signal for firing was given. M. le Pique fired and missed. M. de Grandprè fired and sent a ball through Le Pique's balloon, which collapsed and the car descended with frightful rapidity, and Le Pique and his second were dashed to pieces.

De Grandprè continued his ascent and landed safely at a distance of seven leagues from Paris.

NOVEL & FATAL BALLOON DUEL.

An illustration of the bizarre method of settling a dispute.

CHARLES GREEN

Green was the United Kingdom's most famous aeronaut of the 19th century. In 1821, he made his first ascent in a balloon filled with coal gas instead of the more conventional hydrogen. Coal gas was both cheaper and more readily available, making voyages far more economical. He is also credited with inventing the trail rope as an aid to steering and landing the balloon. To honour his aeronautical career, he has the "Charles Green Salver" trophy named after him. This is awarded by the British Balloon and Airship Club (BBAC) for exceptional achievements and contributions to ballooning.

Portrait of Charles Green by Hilaire Ledru, 1835.

Charles Green's Royal Vauxhall (Nassau) balloon over the Medway on 7th November 1836. In this balloon he set a distance record, in 1836, of 480 miles - a record which stood until 1905.

THE BALLOON AS A SCIENTIFIC INSTRUMENT

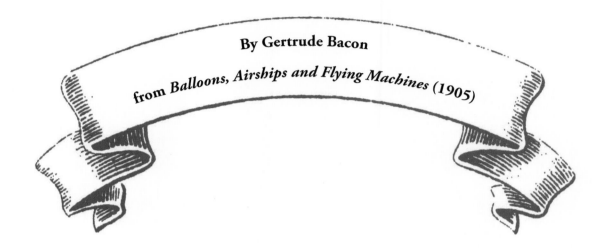

By Gertrude Bacon

from Balloons, Airships and Flying Machines (1905)

The ascent of a balloon was, and still is, an immensely crowd pleasing spectacle, but the importance of the new invention was not just for entertainment, it was also an invaluable aid to the scientific understanding of the atmosphere. For the first time, scientists were able to directly observe and measure meteorological phenomena where they were happening. Up to this point, it had only been theorised what the effects of altitude were, and pioneers like Gay-Lussac tested for everything from electricity to its effects on reptilian anatomy. The following article by Gertrude Bacon, a female English Aeronaut, tells of how the human spirit of curiosity took to the skies.

It is now time to speak of the practical uses of the balloon, and how it has been employed as a most valuable scientific instrument to teach us facts about the upper atmosphere, its nature and extent, the clouds, the winds and their ways, the travel of sounds, and many other things of which we should otherwise be ignorant.

Before the invention of the balloon men were quite unaware of the nature of the air even a short distance above their heads. In those days high mountain climbing had not come into fashion, and when Pilâtre de Rozier made the first ascent, it was considered very doubtful whether he might be able to exist in the strange atmosphere aloft. Charles and Roberts were the first to make scientific observations from a balloon, for they took up a thermometer and barometer, and made certain rough records, as also did other early aeronauts. The most interesting purely scientific ascents of early days, however, were made in the autumn of 1804, from Paris, by Gay Lussac, a famous French philosopher. He took up with him all manner of instruments, among them a compass (to see if the needle behaved the same as on earth), an apparatus to test the electricity of the air, thermometers,

Joseph Louis Gay-Lussac (1778-1850)

Gay-Lussac was a notable French chemist and physicist who is mostly known for his work on gases and alcohol-water mixtures. In 1802 he formulated the law, 'Gay-Lussac's Law', stating that if the mass and volume of a gas are held constant then gas pressure increases linearly as the temperature rises. He also recognised iodine as a new element, was the co-discoverer of boron, and has the measuring scale 'Degrees Gay-Lussac' (units of measuring alcohol-water mixtures used to measure alcoholic beverages in many countries) named after him.

barometers, and hygrometers, carefully exhausted flasks in which to bring down samples of the upper air, birds, and even insects and frogs, to see how great heights affected them. In his second voyage his balloon attained the enormous altitude of 23,000 feet, or more than four miles and a quarter, and nearly 2000 feet higher than the highest peaks of the Andes. At this tremendous height the temperature fell to far below freezing-point, and the aeronaut became extremely cold, though warmly clad; he also felt headache, a difficulty in breathing, and his throat became so parched that he could hardly swallow. Nevertheless, undismayed by the awfulness of his position, he continued making his observations, and eventually reached the ground in safety, and none the worse for his experience.

Gay Lussac's experiments at least proved that though the air becomes less and less dense as we ascend into it, it remains of the same nature and constitution. His second voyage also showed that the limit to which man could ascend aloft into the sky and yet live had not yet been reached. Almost sixty years later other scientific ascents threw fresh light on this point, and also continued the other investigations that Gay Lussac had commenced.

Towards the close of Charles Green's famous career, scientific men in England woke up to the fact that the use of a balloon as an important means for obtaining observations on meteorology and other matters had of late been very much neglected. The British Association took the matter up, and provided the money for four scientific ascents, which were made by Mr. Welsh of Kew Observatory, a trained observer. Green was the aeronaut chosen to accompany him, and the balloon used was none other than the great Nassau balloon. Green was then nearly seventy years of age, but his skill as an aeronaut was as great as ever, and Welsh was able to obtain many valuable records. During the last voyage a height was attained almost as great as that reached by Gay Lussac, and both men found much difficulty in breathing. While at this elevation they suddenly noticed they were rapidly approaching the sea, and so were forced to make a very hasty descent, in which many of the instruments were broken.

The veteran Green lived to a ripe old age, dying in 1870, aged eighty-five. When a very old man he still delighted in taking visitors to an outhouse where he kept the old Nassau balloon, now worn out and useless, and, handling it affectionately, would talk of its famous adventures and his own thousand ascents, during which he had never once met with serious accident or failure. After his death the old balloon passed into the hands of another equally famous man, who, after Green's retirement, took his place as the most celebrated English aeronaut of the day.

This was Henry Coxwell. He was the son of a naval officer, and was brought up to the profession of a dentist. But when a boy of only nine years old he watched, through his father's telescope, a balloon ascent by Green, which so fired his imagination that hence-forward balloons filled all his thoughts. As he grew older the fascination increased upon him. He would go long distances to see ascents or catch glimpses of balloons in the air, and he was fortunate enough to be present at the first launching of the great Nassau balloon. He did not get the chance of a voyage aloft, however, till he was twenty-five; but after this nothing could restrain his ardour, and, throwing his profession to the winds, he made ascent after ascent on all possible occasions.

In one of his early voyages he met with what he describes as one of the most perilous descents in the whole history of ballooning. The occasion was an evening ascent made from the Vauxhall Gardens one autumn night of 1848. The aeronaut was a Mr. Gypson, and besides Mr. Coxwell there

Henry Coxwell (1819-1900)

were two other passengers, one of whom was the well-known mountaineer and lecturer, Albert Smith. A number of fireworks which were to be displayed when aloft were slung on a framework forty feet below the car.

The balloon rose high above London, and the party were amazed and delighted with the strange and lovely view of the great city by night, all sight of the houses being lost in the darkness, and the thousands of gas lamps, out-lining the invisible streets and bridges, twinkling like stars in a blue-black sky. Coxwell was sitting, not in the car, but in the ring of the balloon, and presently, when they were about 7000 feet above the town, he noticed that the silk, the mouth of which appears to have been fastened, was growing dangerously distended with the expanding gas. By his advice the valve was immediately pulled, but it was already too late; the balloon burst,

This stamp commemorates one hundred years since the first official airmail delivery by the U.S Post Office, in 1859. The Jupiter, piloted by American balloonist John Wise, set off in the summer of 1859 from Lafayette, Indiana, with the intention of reaching New York. He ascended with a cargo of 123 letters from Lafayette citizens, but unfortunately the winds were not in his favour and he was forced to land 30 miles south of the city. The Postal Service however, honoured their commitment and took the letters the rest of the way by train.

the gas escaped with a noise like the escape of steam from an engine, the silk collapsed, and the balloon began to descend with appalling speed, the immense mass of loose silk surging and rustling frightfully overhead. Everything was immediately thrown out of the car to break the fall; but the wind still seemed to be rushing past at a fearful rate, and, to add to the horror of the aeronauts, they now came down through the remains of the discharged fireworks floating in the air. Little bits of burning cases and still smouldering touch-paper blew about them, and were caught in the rigging. These kindled into sparks, and there seemed every chance of the whole balloon catching alight. They were still a whole mile from the ground, and this distance they appear to have covered in less than two minutes. The house-tops seemed advancing up towards them with awful speed as they neared earth. In the end they were tossed out of the car along the ground, and it appeared a perfect marvel to them all that they escaped with only a severe shaking. This adventure did not in the least abate Coxwell's ardour for ballooning, and exactly a week later he and Gypson successfully made the same ascent from the same place, and in the same balloon — and loaded with twice the number of fireworks!

But Coxwell's most celebrated voyage of all took place some years later, on the occasion of a scientific voyage made in company with Mr. James Glaisher. In 1862 the British Association determined to continue the balloon observations which Mr. Welsh had so successfully commenced, but this time on a larger scale. The observer was to be Mr. Glaisher of Greenwich Observatory, and Mr. Coxwell, who by this time had become a recognised aeronaut, undertook the management of the balloon. The first ascents were made in July and August. Mr. Glaisher took up a most elaborate and costly outfit of instruments, which, however, were badly damaged at the outset during a very rapid descent, made per-force to avoid falling in the " Wash." On each occasion a height of over four miles was attained; but on the third voyage, which was in September, it was decided to try and reach yet greater altitudes.

The balloon with its two passengers left Wolverhampton at 1 p.m. — the temperature on the ground being 59°. At about a mile high a dense cloud was entered, and the thermometer fell to 36°. In nineteen minutes a height of two miles was reached, and the air was at freezing-point. Six minutes later they were three miles aloft, with the thermometer still falling ; and by the time four miles high was attained the mercury registered only 8°.

In forty-seven minutes from the start five miles had been passed; and now the temperature was 2° below zero. Mr. Coxwell, who was up in the ring of the balloon and exerting himself over the management of it, found he was beginning to breathe with great difficulty. Mr. Glaisher, sitting quietly in the car watching his instruments, felt no inconvenience. More ballast was thrown out, and the balloon continued to rise apace; and soon Mr. Glaisher found his eyes growing strangely dim. He could not see to read his thermometer, or distinguish the hands of his watch. He noticed the mercury of the barometer, however, and saw that a height of 29,000 feet had been reached, and the balloon was still rising. What followed next had best be told in Mr. Glaisher's own words : — "Shortly after I laid my arm upon the table, possessed of its full vigour, but on being desirous of using it, I found it useless. Trying to move the other arm, I found it powerless also. Then I tried to shake myself and succeeded, but I seemed to have no limbs. In looking at the barometer my head fell over my left shoulder. I struggled and shook my body again, but could not move my arms.

"Getting my head upright for an instant only, it fell on my right shoulder; then I fell backwards, my body resting against the side of the car, and my head on the edge. I dimly saw Mr. Coxwell and endeavoured to speak, but could not. In an instant intense darkness overcame me; but I was still conscious, with as active a brain as at the present moment while writing this. I thought I had been seized with asphyxia, and believed I should experience nothing more, as death would come unless we speedily descended. Other thoughts were entering my mind, when I suddenly became unconscious as on going to sleep." Mr. Glaisher adds: "I cannot tell anything of the sense of hearing, as no sound reaches the ear to break the perfect stillness and silence of the regions between six and seven miles above the earth."

Meanwhile, as stated, Mr. Coxwell was up in the ring, trying to secure the valve-line, which had become twisted. To do this he had taken off a pair of thick gloves he had been wearing, and in the tremendous cold of that awful region the moment his bare hands rested on the metal of the ring they became frost-bitten and useless. Looking down, he saw Mr. Glaisher in a fainting condition, and called out to him, but received no answer. Thoroughly alarmed by this time, he tried to come down to his companion's assistance; but now his hands also had become lifeless, and he felt unconsciousness rapidly stealing over him.

Quickly realising that death to both of them would speedily follow if the balloon continued to ascend, Mr. Coxwell now endeavoured to pull the valve-line; but he found it impossible to do so with

Coxwell and Glaisher's perilous voyage on 5th September 1862.

James Glaisher (1809-1903)

his disabled hands. Fortunately he was a man of great bodily strength, as well as of iron nerve, and by a great effort he succeeded in catching the valve-line in his teeth. Then, putting his whole weight upon it, he managed to pull open the valve, and hold it until the balloon took a decided turn downwards. This saved them. As lower regions were reached, where the air was denser, Mr. Glaisher began to recover, and by the time they came to the ground neither of these two brave men were any the worse for their extraordinary experience.

Neither Mr. Glaisher or Mr. Coxwell were able to note the exact elevation when they were at their greatest height; but from several circumstances they were convinced that it must have been 36,000 or 37,000 feet, or fully seven miles high. Later aeronauts have been inclined to doubt if this surmise can be quite correct; but whether it is so or not is of no great moment, for this great balloon ascent will always stand unrivalled in the history of ballooning. Since that day nearly as great, or perhaps even greater, heights have been reached in balloons; but nowadays those who attempt to ascend to great elevations always provide themselves, before they start, with cylinders of com-pressed oxygen gas. Then when the atmosphere aloft becomes so thin and rare as to make breathing difficult, they begin to fill their lungs with the life-giving gas from the cylinders, and at once recover.

After this perilous voyage Glaisher and Coxwell made several other scientific balloon ascents. They met with various experiences. On one occasion, during a lofty ascent, they lost sight of the earth above the clouds for a while, but, the mist suddenly breaking, they found themselves on the point of drifting out to sea. Not a moment was to be lost, and both men hung on to the valve-line until it cut their hands. The result was a tremendously rapid descent. The balloon fell four and a quarter miles in less than a quarter of an hour, covering the last two miles in only four minutes. They reached earth close to the shore, and were fortunate to escape with only a few bruises, though all the instruments were once more broken in the shock.

Mr. Glaisher was able to make many interesting notes of the condition of the winds and clouds at high levels. He observed how frequently different currents of air are blowing aloft in different directions at the same time. These differing winds affect the shape of the clouds among which they blow. High above the ground he frequently met with a warm wind blowing constantly from the south-west; and he believed that it is largely due to this mild air-stream passing always overhead that England enjoys such much less rigorous winters than other countries that lie as far north of the equator. This mildness of our climate has long been attributed to the Gulf Stream, that warm current of the sea which sweeps up from the tropics past our shores. But it may well be that there is besides an " Aerial Gulf Stream," as Mr. Glaisher calls it, blowing constantly above our heads, which also serves to warm the air, and make our winter climate mild and moist.

One fact these experiments seemed to establish was, that when rain is falling from an overcast sky, there is always a higher layer of clouds overhanging the lower stratum. Nothing surprised Mr. Glaisher more than the extreme rapidity with which the whole sky, up to a vast height, could fill up entirely with clouds at the approach of a storm. Another point noted was that, when a wind is blowing, the upper portion of the current always travels faster than that next the ground. This is due, of course, to the obstacles the wind meets as it sweeps over the earth, and which check its onward progress.

These, and very many other facts of the greatest interest to the meteorologist, were the outcome of Mr. Glaisher's experiments. Later voyages of a similar kind have added greatly to our knowledge of the condition of the air, and it seems certain that in the future the balloon will be much more used by scientific men, and by its means they will be able to predict the weather more accurately and further ahead than at present, and learn many other things of which we are now in ignorance.

THE ZENITH

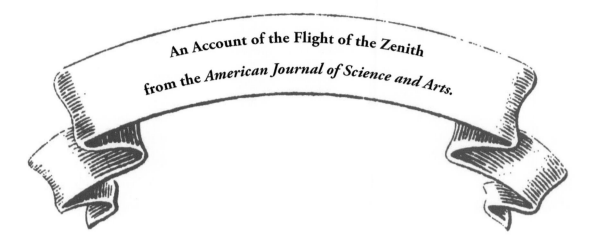

An Account of the Flight of the Zenith from the *American Journal of Science and Arts.*

Gaston Tissandier was a French chemist, meteorologist, and aeronaut. After an eventful first voyage in 1868, in which he and Claude-Jules Duruof were blown over the North Sea, barely making it back to the coast, Tissandier became hooked on ballooning and made many further ascents. He used the ascents to make scientific observations on optical and atmospheric phenomena, adding much to the field of meteorology. Along with its scientific uses, he also found the balloon a useful method for escape. During the Siege of Paris (1870-1871), Tissandier and a number of other aviators were trapped in the French capital. They formed a plan with the government to reopen lines of communication with the outside world by taking to the skies and delivering letters beyond the enemy barricades. This proved a successful concept, with 3 million letters being delivered by the brave aeronauts.

Tissansdier's most famous voyage is that of the Zenith in 1875. He and two others, Croce-Spinelli and Sivel, set out to try and topple the altitude record set by James Glaisher in 1862. Glaisher had nearly lost his life during the previous flight, but Tissandier and his colleagues believed their preparations and oxygen supply would hold them in good stead. The ascent ended in tragedy, with only Tissandier making it out alive. The following article is a contemporary account of the flight of the Zenith from the American Journal of Science and Arts.

On the morning of the 16th of April last, under the auspices of the Academy of Sciences, the Zenith, containing the three experienced aeronauts, Captain Sivel, Croce-Spinelli and Gaston Tissandier, and well equipped for scientific work, started on its ascent from the gas works of La Villette, Paris. By 1 o'clock, at noon, they had reached an altitude exceeding 5,000 meters, the barometer marking a pressure of 400 millimeters, and the thermometer 5° C. They had oxygen in bags for breathing in the upper rarefied air, and found it very beneficial At 1h 20 the barometer marked 320 mm., showing an altitude of 7,000 meters; the temperature was -10° C., and soon afterward 7,400, with the temperature -11° C. Sivel and Croce were already pale and very feeble. By mutual consent Sivel

The Fatal voyage of the Zenith.

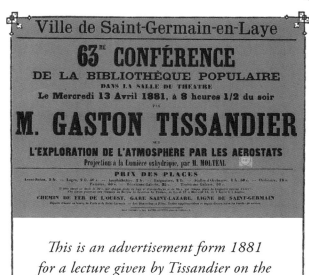

This is an advertisement form 1881 for a lecture given by Tissandier on the exploration of the atmosphere by balloon.

with his knife cut the cords which kept closed three sacs of ballast of 25 kilograms each that were hanging outside. The three sacs emptying themselves, the balloon ascended rapidly, and near 1h 30 all three of the aeronauts bad fainted. Tissandier, as his consciousness was leaving him, read from the barometer 280 mm., but was already too much paralyzed to speak out his thought– 8,000 meters. Tissandier and his friends partially revived, as the balloon was making a very rapid descent; but again all became asphyxiated. The survivor supposes that more ballast was probably dropped by one of them to prevent a fatal descent, and up the balloon went. At 3 o'clock the balloon was again descending rapidly, and Tissandier became conscious; and at 4 o'clock it struck the earth at Ciron near Le Blanche with a severe shock. Sivel and Croce were dead, their faces black and their mouths full of blood. The greatest height reached, as indicated by the self-registering barometer, was 8,540 to 8,600 meters. The lessons taught to science are: that man cannot safely make a rapid balloon ascent to an altitude of 8,000 meters; that the only chance for reaching alive that altitude in a balloon is by making the rate of ascent above 7,000 meters very slow, giving 12 hours at least to the next 1,000 meters, and a rate half as fast for the meters beyond; that better arrangements for carrying up air or oxygen to supply the breathers may be of service; that man reaches soon the upward limit of atmospheric investigation.

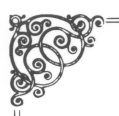

THE BALLOON HOAX

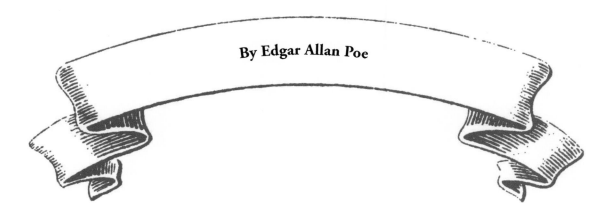

By Edgar Allan Poe

In 1844, the following article, now known as 'The Balloon Hoax', was printed as a true story in 'The Sun' newspaper in New York. Such was the excitement and optimism in ballooning at the time, that a story detailing a crossing of the Atlantic seemed highly plausible. Poe also included real people, including William Harrison Ainsworth, a novelist, to make the story even more convincing. It would turn out to be over one hundred years until this feat was achieved in reality.

ASTOUNDING NEWS BY EXPRESS, VIA NORFOLK! – The Atlantic Crossed in Three Days! – Signal Triumph of Mr. Monck Mason's Flying Machine! – Arrival at Sullivan's Island, near Charlestown, S. C., of Mr. Mason, Mr. Robert Holland, Mr. Henson, Mr. Harrison Ainsworth, and four others, in the Steering Balloon, Victoria, after a Passage of Seventy-five Hours from Land to Land! Full Particulars of the Voyage!

The subjoined jeu d'esprit with the preceding heading in magnificent capitals, well interspersed with notes of admiration, was originally published, as matter of fact, in the New York Sun, a daily newspaper, and therein fully subserved the purpose of creating indigestible aliment for the quidnuncs during the few hours intervening between a couple of the Charleston mails. The rush for the "sole paper which had the news" was something beyond even the prodigious; and, in fact, if (as some assert) the Victoria did not absolutely accomplish the voyage recorded it will be difficult to assign a reason why she should not have accomplished it. E. A. P.

THE great problem is at length solved! The air, as well as the earth and the ocean, has been subdued by science, and will become a common and convenient highway for mankind. *The Atlantic has been actually crossed in a Balloon!* and this too without difficulty—without any great apparent danger—with thorough control of the machine—and in the inconceivably brief period of seventy-five hours from shore to shore! By the energy of an agent at Charleston, S.C., we are enabled to be the first to furnish the public with a detailed account of this most extraordinary voyage, which was performed between Saturday, the 6th instant, at 11, A.M., and 2, P.M., on Tuesday, the 9th instant, by Sir Everard Bringhurst; Mr. Osborne, a nephew of Lord Bentinck's; Mr. Monck Mason and Mr. Robert Holland, the well-known æronauts; Mr. Harrison Ainsworth, author of "Jack Sheppard," &c.; and Mr. Henson, the projector of the late unsuccessful flying machine—with two seamen from Woolwich—in all, eight persons. The particulars furnished below may be relied on as authentic and accurate in every respect, as, with a slight exception, they are copied *verbatim* from the joint diaries of Mr. Monck Mason and Mr. Harrison Ainsworth, to whose politeness our agent is also indebted for much verbal information respecting the balloon itself, its construction, and other matters of interest. The only alteration in the MS. received, has been made for the purpose of throwing the hurried account of our agent, Mr. Forsyth, into a connected and intelligible form.

Edgar Allan Poe (1809-1849)

THE BALLOON

"Two very decided failures, of late—those of Mr. Henson and Sir George Cayley—had much weakened the public interest in the subject of aerial navigation. Mr. Henson's scheme (which at first was considered very feasible even by men of science,) was founded upon the principle of an inclined plane, started from an eminence by an extrinsic force, applied and continued by the revolution of impinging vanes, in form and number resembling the vanes of a windmill. But, in all the experiments made with models at the Adelaide Gallery, it was found that the operation of these fans not only did not propel the machine, but actually impeded its flight. The only propelling force it ever exhibited, was the mere *impetus* acquired from the descent of the inclined plane; and this *impetus* carried the machine farther when the vanes were at rest, than when they were in motion—a fact which sufficiently demonstrates their inutility; and in the absence of the propelling, which was also the *sustaining* power, the whole fabric would necessarily descend. This consideration led Sir George Cayley to think only of adapting a propeller to some machine having of itself an independent power of support—in a word, to a balloon; the idea, however, being novel, or original, with Sir George, only so far as regards the mode of its application to practice. He exhibited a model of his invention at the Polytechnic Institution. The propelling principle, or power, was here, also, applied to interrupted surfaces, or vanes, put in revolution. These vanes were four in number, but were found entirely ineffectual in moving the balloon, or in aiding its ascending power. The whole project was thus a complete failure.

"It was at this juncture that Mr. Monck Mason (whose voyage from Dover to Weilburg in the balloon, "Nassau," occasioned so much excitement in 1837,) conceived the idea of employing the principle of the Archimedean screw for the purpose of propulsion through the air—rightly attributing the failure of Mr. Henson's scheme, and of Sir George Cayley's, to the interruption of surface in the independent vanes. He made the first public experiment at Willis's Rooms, but afterward removed his model to the Adelaide Gallery.

"Like Sir George Cayley's balloon, his own was an ellipsoid. Its length was thirteen feet six inches—height, six feet eight inches. It contained about three hundred and twenty cubic feet of gas, which, if pure hydrogen, would support twenty-one pounds upon its first inflation, before the gas has time to deteriorate or escape. The weight of the whole machine and apparatus was seventeen pounds—leaving about four pounds to spare. Beneath the centre of the balloon, was a frame of light wood, about nine feet long, and rigged on to the balloon itself with a network in the customary manner. From this framework was suspended a wicker basket or car.

"The screw consists of an axis of hollow brass tube, eighteen inches in length, through which, upon a semi-spiral inclined at fifteen degrees, pass a series of steel wire radii, two feet long, and thus projecting a foot on either side. These radii are connected at the outer extremities by two bands of flattened wire—the whole in this manner forming the framework of the screw, which is completed by a covering of oiled silk cut into gores, and tightened so as to present a tolerably uniform surface. At each end of its axis this screw is supported by pillars of hollow brass tube descending from the hoop. In the lower ends of these tubes are holes in which the pivots of the axis revolve. From the end of the axis which is next the car, proceeds a shaft of steel, connecting the screw with the pinion of a piece of spring machinery fixed in the car. By the operation of this spring, the screw is made to revolve with great rapidity, communicating a progressive motion to the whole. By means of the rudder, the machine was readily turned in any direction. The spring was of great power, compared with its dimensions, being capable of raising forty-five pounds upon a barrel of four inches diameter, after the first turn, and gradually increasing as it was wound up. It weighed, altogether, eight pounds six ounces. The rudder was a light frame of cane covered with silk, shaped somewhat like a battle-door, and was about three feet long, and at the widest, one foot. Its weight was about two ounces. It could be turned *flat*, and directed upwards or downwards, as well as to the right or left; and thus enabled the æronaut to transfer the resistance of the air which in an inclined position it must generate in its passage, to any side upon which he might desire to act; thus determining the balloon in the opposite direction.

"This model (which, through want of time, we have necessarily described in an imperfect manner,) was put in action at the Adelaide Gallery, where it accomplished a velocity of five miles per hour;

although, strange to say, it excited very little interest in comparison with the previous complex machine of Mr. Henson—so resolute is the world to despise anything which carries with it an air of simplicity. To accomplish the great desideratum of ærial navigation, it was very generally supposed that some exceedingly complicated application must be made of some unusually profound principle in dynamics.

"So well satisfied, however, was Mr. Mason of the ultimate success of his invention, that he determined to construct immediately, if possible, a balloon of sufficient capacity to test the question by a voyage of some extent—the original design being to cross the British Channel, as before, in the Nassau balloon. To carry out his views, he solicited and obtained the patronage of Sir Everard Bringhurst and Mr. Osborne, two gentlemen well known for scientific acquirement, and especially for the interest they have exhibited in the progress of ærostation. The project, at the desire of Mr. Osborne, was kept a profound secret from the public—the only persons entrusted with the design being those actually engaged in the construction of the machine, which was built (under

"The Balloon Hoax" as it appeared in The Sun *newspaper (1844).*

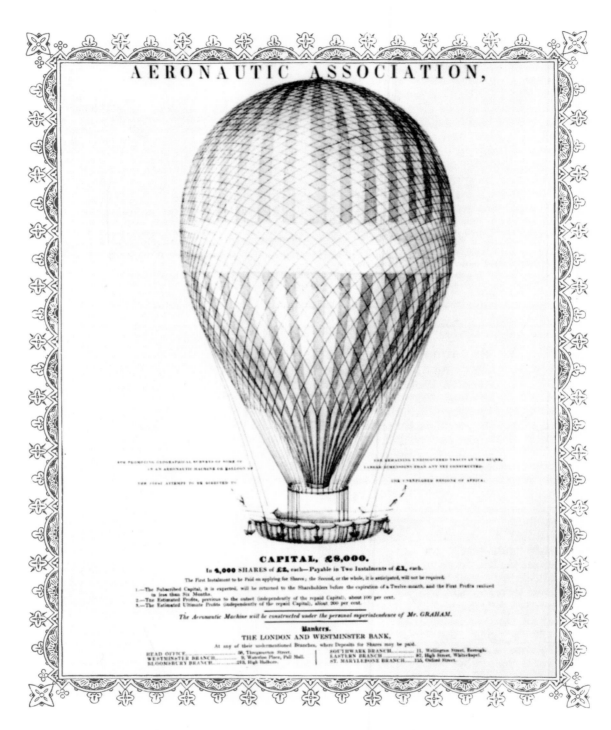

An advert offering the chance to buy shares in a balloon to survey "the remaining undiscovered tracts of the globe."

the superintendence of Mr. Mason, Mr. Holland, Sir Everard Bringhurst, and Mr. Osborne,) at the seat of the latter gentleman near Penstruthal, in Wales. Mr. Henson, accompanied by his friend Mr. Ainsworth, was admitted to a private view of the balloon, on Saturday last—when the two gentlemen made final arrangements to be included in the adventure. We are not informed for what reason the two seamen were also included in the party—but, in the course of a day or two, we shall put our readers in possession of the minutest particulars respecting this extraordinary voyage.

"The balloon is composed of silk, varnished with the liquid gum caoutchouc. It is of vast dimensions, containing more than 40,000 cubic feet of gas; but as coal gas was employed in place of the more expensive and inconvenient hydrogen, the supporting power of the machine, when fully inflated, and immediately after inflation, is not more than about 2500 pounds. The coal gas is not only much less costly, but is easily procured and managed.

"For its introduction into common use for purposes of aerostation, we are indebted to Mr. Charles Green. Up to his discovery, the process of inflation was not only exceedingly expensive, but uncertain. Two, and even three days, have frequently been wasted in futile attempts to procure a sufficiency of hydrogen to fill a balloon, from which it had great tendency to escape, owing to its extreme subtlety, and its affinity for the surrounding atmosphere. In a balloon sufficiently perfect to retain its contents of coal-gas unaltered, in quantity or amount, for six months, an equal quantity of hydrogen could not be maintained in equal purity for six weeks.

"The supporting power being estimated at 2500 pounds, and the united weights of the party amounting only to about 1200, there was left a surplus of 1300, of which again 1200 was exhausted by ballast, arranged in bags of different sizes, with their respective weights marked upon them—by cordage, barometers, telescopes, barrels containing provision for a fortnight, water-casks, cloaks, carpet-bags, and various other indispensable matters, including a coffee-warmer, contrived for warming coffee by means of slack-lime, so as to dispense altogether with fire, if it should be judged prudent to do so. All these articles, with the exception of the ballast, and a few trifles, were suspended from the hoop overhead. The car is much smaller and lighter, in proportion, than the one appended to the model. It is formed of a light wicker, and is wonderfully strong, for so frail looking a machine. Its rim is about four feet deep. The rudder is also very much larger, in proportion, than that of the model; and the screw is considerably smaller. The balloon is furnished besides with a grapnel, and a guide-rope; which latter is of the most indispensable importance. A few words, in explanation, will here be necessary for such of our readers as are not conversant with the details of aerostation.

"As soon as the balloon quits the earth, it is subjected to the influence of many circumstances tending to create a difference in its weight; augmenting or diminishing its ascending power. For example, there may be a deposition of dew upon the silk, to the extent, even, of several hundred pounds; ballast has then to be thrown out, or the machine may descend. This ballast being discarded, and a clear sunshine evaporating the dew, and at the same time expanding the gas in the silk, the whole will again rapidly ascend. To check this ascent, the only recourse is, (or rather *was*, until Mr. Green's invention of the guide-rope,) the permission of the escape of gas from the valve; but, in

Thomas Monck Mason (1803-1889) (on the far right). Monck Mason in Poe's story is based on Thomas Monck Mason and his 'Account of the Late æronautical Expedition from London to Weilburg'. This work detailed his 1836 trip with Charles Green and Robert Hollond from Dover, England, to Weilburg in Nassau, a distance record of 500 miles. The painting above, by John Hollins, is called 'A Consultation Prior to the Aerial Voyage to Weilburgh, 1836', and includes from left to right: Walter Prideaux, John Hollins (the artist), M.P. Sir William Milbourne James, Robert Hollond, Charles Green, and Thomas Monck Mason.

the loss of gas, is a proportionate general loss of ascending power; so that, in a comparatively brief period, the best-constructed balloon must necessarily exhaust all its resources, and come to the earth. This was the great obstacle to voyages of length.

"The guide-rope remedies the difficulty in the simplest manner conceivable. It is merely a very long rope which is suffered to trail from the car, and the effect of which is to prevent the balloon from changing its level in any material degree. If, for example, there should be a deposition of moisture upon the silk, and the machine begins to descend in consequence, there will be no necessity for discharging ballast to remedy the increase of weight, for it is remedied, or counteracted, in an exactly just proportion, by the deposit on the ground of just so much of the end of the rope as is necessary. If, on the other hand, any circumstances should cause undue levity, and consequent ascent, this levity is immediately counteracted by the additional weight of rope upraised from the earth. Thus, the balloon can neither ascend or descend, except within very narrow limits, and its resources, either in gas or ballast, remain comparatively unimpaired. When passing over an expanse of water, it becomes necessary to employ small kegs of copper or wood, filled with liquid ballast of a lighter nature than water. These float, and serve all the purposes of a mere rope on land. Another most important office of the guide-rope, is to point out the *direction* of the balloon. The rope *drags*, either on land or sea, while the balloon is free; the latter, consequently, is always in advance, when any progress whatever is made: a comparison, therefore, by means of the compass, of the relative positions of the two objects, will always indicate the *course*. In the same way, the angle formed by the rope with the vertical axis of the machine, indicates the *velocity*. When there is *no* angle—in other words, when the rope hangs perpendicularly, the whole apparatus is stationary; but the larger the angle, that is to say, the farther the balloon precedes the end of the rope, the greater the velocity; and the converse.

"As the original design was to cross the British Channel, and alight as near Paris as possible, the voyagers had taken the precaution to prepare themselves with passports directed to all parts of the Continent, specifying the nature of the expedition, as in the case of the Nassau voyage, and entitling the adventurers to exemption from the usual formalities of office: unexpected events, however, rendered these passports superfluous.

"The inflation was commenced very quietly at daybreak, on Saturday morning, the 6th instant, in the Court-Yard of Weal-Vor House, Mr. Osborne's seat, about a mile from Penstruthal, in North Wales; and at 7 minutes past 11, every thing being ready for departure, the balloon was set free, rising gently but steadily, in a direction nearly South; no use being made, for the first half hour, of either the screw or the rudder. We proceed now with the journal, as transcribed by Mr. Forsyth from the joint MSS. of Mr. Monck Mason, and Mr. Ainsworth. The body of the journal, as given, is in the hand-writing of Mr. Mason, and a P. S. is appended, each day, by Mr. Ainsworth, who has in preparation, and will shortly give the public a more minute, and no doubt, a thrillingly interesting account of the voyage.

THE JOURNAL

"*Saturday, April the 6th.*—Every preparation likely to embarrass us, having been made over night, we commenced the inflation this morning at daybreak; but owing to a thick fog, which encumbered the folds of the silk and rendered it unmanageable, we did not get through before nearly eleven o'clock. Cut loose, then, in high spirits, and rose gently but steadily, with a light breeze at North, which bore us in the direction of the British Channel. Found the ascending force greater than we had expected; and as we arose higher and so got clear of the cliffs, and more in the sun's rays, our ascent became very rapid. I did not wish, however, to lose gas at so early a period of the adventure, and so concluded to ascend for the present. We soon ran out our guide-rope; but even when we had raised it clear of the earth, we still went up very rapidly. The balloon was unusually steady, and looked beautifully. In about ten minutes after starting, the barometer indicated an altitude of 15,000 feet. The weather was remarkably fine, and the view of the subjacent country—a most romantic one when seen from any point,—was now especially sublime. The numerous deep gorges presented the appearance of lakes, on account of the dense vapors with which they were filled, and the pinnacles and crags to the South East, piled in inextricable confusion, resembling nothing so much as the giant cities of eastern fable. We were rapidly approaching the mountains in the South; but our elevation was more than sufficient to enable us to pass them in safety. In a few minutes we soared over them in fine style; and Mr. Ainsworth, with the seamen, was surprised at their apparent want of altitude when viewed from the car, the tendency of great elevation in a balloon being to reduce inequalities of the surface below, to nearly a dead level. At half-past eleven still proceeding nearly South, we obtained our first view of the Bristol Channel; and, in fifteen minutes afterward, the line of breakers on the coast appeared immediately beneath us, and we were fairly out at sea. We now resolved to let off enough gas to bring our guide-rope, with the buoys affixed, into the water. This was immediately done, and we commenced a gradual descent. In about twenty minutes our first buoy dipped, and at the touch of the second soon afterwards, we remained stationary as to elevation. We were all now anxious to test the efficiency of the rudder and screw, and we put them both into requisition forthwith, for the purpose of altering our direction more to the eastward, and in a line for Paris. By means of the rudder we instantly effected the necessary change of direction, and our course was brought nearly at right angles to that of the wind; when we set in motion the spring of the screw, and were rejoiced to find it propel us readily as desired. Upon this we gave nine hearty cheers, and dropped in the sea a bottle, enclosing a slip of parchment with a brief account of the principle of the invention. Hardly, however, had we done with our rejoicings, when an unforeseen accident occurred which discouraged us in no little degree. The steel rod connecting the spring with the propeller was suddenly jerked out of place, at the car end, (by a swaying of the car through some movement of one of the two seamen we had taken up,) and in an instant hung dangling out of reach, from the pivot of the axis of the screw. While we were endeavoring to regain it, our attention being completely absorbed, we became involved in a strong current of wind from the East, which bore us, with rapidly

VOYAGE A LA LUNE.

A comical illustration of a flying machine from the mid 19th century.

increasing force, towards the Atlantic. We soon found ourselves driving out to sea at the rate of not less, certainly, than fifty or sixty miles an hour, so that we came up with Cape Clear, at some forty miles to our North, before we had secured the rod, and had time to think what we were about. It was now that Mr. Ainsworth made an extraordinary, but to my fancy, a by no means unreasonable or chimerical proposition, in which he was instantly seconded by Mr. Holland—viz.: that we should take advantage of the strong gale which bore us on, and in place of beating back to Paris, make an attempt to reach the coast of North America. After slight reflection I gave a willing assent to this bold proposition, which (strange to say) met with objection from the two seamen only. As the stronger party, however, we overruled their fears, and kept resolutely upon our course. We steered due West; but as the trailing of the buoys materially impeded our progress, and we had the balloon abundantly at command, either for ascent or descent, we first threw out fifty pounds of ballast, and then wound up (by means of a windlass) so much of the rope as brought it quite clear of the sea. We perceived the effect of this manoeuvre immediately, in a vastly increased rate of progress; and, as the gale freshened, we flew with a velocity nearly inconceivable; the guide-rope flying out behind the car, like a streamer from a vessel. It is needless to say that a very short time sufficed us to lose sight of the coast. We passed over innumerable vessels of all kinds, a few of which were endeavoring to beat up, but the most of them lying to. We occasioned the greatest excitement on board all—an excitement greatly relished by ourselves, and especially by our two men, who, now under the influence of a dram of Geneva, seemed resolved to give all scruple, or fear, to the wind. Many of the vessels fired signal guns; and in all we were saluted with loud cheers (which we heard with surprising distinctness) and the waving of caps and handkerchiefs. We kept on in this manner throughout the day, with no material incident, and, as the shades of night closed around us, we made a rough estimate of the distance traversed. It could not have been less than five hundred miles, and was probably much more. The propeller was kept in constant operation, and, no doubt, aided our progress materially.

As the sun went down, the gale freshened into an absolute hurricane, and the ocean beneath was clearly visible on account of its phosphorescence. The wind was from the East all night, and gave us the brightest omen of success. We suffered no little from cold, and the dampness of the atmosphere was most unpleasant; but the ample space in the car enabled us to lie down, and by means of cloaks and a few blankets, we did sufficiently well.

"P.S. (by Mr. Ainsworth.) The last nine hours have been unquestionably the most exciting of my life. I can conceive nothing more sublimating than the strange peril and novelty of an adventure such as this. May God grant that we succeed! I ask not success for mere safety to my insignificant person, but for the sake of human knowledge and—for the vastness of the triumph. And yet the feat is only so evidently feasible that the sole wonder is why men have scrupled to attempt it before. One single gale such as now befriends us—let such a tempest whirl forward a balloon for four or five days (these gales often last longer) and the voyager will be easily borne, in that period, from coast to coast. In view of such a gale the broad Atlantic becomes a mere lake. I am more struck, just now, with the supreme silence which reigns in the sea beneath us, notwithstanding its agitation, than with any other phenomenon presenting itself. The waters give up no voice to the heavens. The immense flaming ocean writhes and is tortured uncomplainingly. The mountainous surges suggest the idea of innumerable dumb gigantic fiends struggling in impotent agony. In a night such as is this to me, a man *lives*—lives a whole century of ordinary life—nor would I forego this rapturous delight for that of a whole century of ordinary existence.

"*Sunday, the seventh.* [Mr. Mason's MS.] This morning the gale, by 10, had subsided to an eight or nine—knot breeze, (for a vessel at sea,) and bears us, perhaps, thirty miles per hour, or more. It has veered, however, very considerably to the north; and now, at sundown, we are holding our course due west, principally by the screw and rudder, which answer their purposes to admiration. I regard the project as thoroughly successful, and the easy navigation of the air in any direction (not exactly in the teeth of a gale) as no longer problematical. We could not have made head against the strong wind of yesterday; but, by ascending, we might have got out of its influence, if requisite. Against a pretty stiff breeze, I feel convinced, we can make our way with the propeller. At noon, to-day, ascended to an elevation of nearly 25,000 feet, by discharging ballast. Did this to search for a more direct current, but found none so favorable as the one we are now in. We have an abundance of gas to take us across this small pond, even should the voyage last three weeks. I have not the slightest fear for the result. The difficulty has been strangely exaggerated and misapprehended. I can choose my current, and should I find *all* currents against me, I can make very tolerable headway with the propeller. We have had no incidents worth recording. The night promises fair.

P.S. [By Mr. Ainsworth.] I have little to record, except the fact (to me quite a surprising one) that, at an elevation equal to that of Cotopaxi, I experienced neither very intense cold, nor headache, nor difficulty of breathing; neither, I find, did Mr. Mason, nor Mr. Holland, nor Sir Everard. Mr. Osborne complained of constriction of the chest—but this soon wore off. We have flown at a great rate during the day, and we must be more than half way across the Atlantic. We have passed over some twenty or thirty vessels of various kinds, and all seem to be delightfully astonished. Crossing the ocean in a balloon is not so difficult a feat after all. *Omne ignotum pro magnifico. Mem:* at 25,000 feet elevation the sky appears nearly black, and the stars are distinctly visible; while the sea does not seem convex (as one might suppose) but absolutely and most unequivocally *concave.*(*1)

"*Monday, the 8th.* [Mr. Mason's MS.] This morning we had again some little trouble with the rod of the propeller, which must be entirely remodelled, for fear of serious accident—I mean the steel rod—not the vanes. The latter could not be improved. The wind has been blowing steadily and strongly from the north-east all day and so far fortune seems bent upon favoring us. Just before day, we were all somewhat alarmed at some odd noises and concussions in the balloon, accompanied with the apparent rapid subsidence of the whole machine. These phenomena were occasioned by the expansion of the gas, through increase of heat in the atmosphere, and the consequent disruption of the minute particles of ice with which the network had become encrusted during the night. Threw down several bottles to the vessels below. Saw one of them picked up by a large ship—seemingly one of the New York line packets. Endeavored to make out her name, but could not be sure of it. Mr. Osborne's telescope made it out something like "Atalanta." It is now 12, at night, and we are still going nearly west, at a rapid pace. The sea is peculiarly phosphorescent.

"P.S. [By Mr. Ainsworth.] It is now 2, A.M., and nearly calm, as well as I can judge—but it is very difficult to determine this point, since we move *with* the air so completely. I have not slept since quitting Wheal-Vor, but can stand it no longer, and must take a nap. We cannot be far from the American coast.

"*Tuesday, the 9th.* [Mr. Ainsworth's MS.] *One, P.M. We are in full view of the low coast of South Carolina.* The great problem is accomplished. We have crossed the Atlantic—fairly and *easily* crossed it in a balloon! God be praised! Who shall say that anything is impossible hereafter?"

The Journal here ceases. Some particulars of the descent were communicated, however, by Mr. Ainsworth to Mr. Forsyth. It was nearly dead calm when the voyagers first came in view of the coast, which was immediately recognized by both the seamen, and by Mr. Osborne. The latter gentleman having acquaintances at Fort Moultrie, it was immediately resolved to descend in its vicinity. The balloon was brought over the beach (the tide being out and the sand hard, smooth, and admirably adapted for a descent,) and the grapnel let go, which took firm hold at once. The inhabitants of the island, and of the fort, thronged out, of course, to see the balloon; but it was with the greatest difficulty that any one could be made to credit the actual voyage—*the crossing of the Atlantic.* The grapnel caught at 2, P.M., precisely; and thus the whole voyage was completed in seventy-five hours; or rather less, counting from shore to shore. No serious accident occurred. No real danger was at any time apprehended. The balloon was exhausted and secured without trouble; and when the MS. from which this narrative is compiled was despatched from Charleston, the party were still at Fort Moultrie. Their farther intentions were not ascertained; but we can safely promise our readers some additional information either on Monday or in the course of the next day, at farthest.

This is unquestionably the most stupendous, the most interesting, and the most important undertaking, ever accomplished or even attempted by man. What magnificent events may ensue, it would be useless now to think of determining.

(*1) *Note.*—Mr. Ainsworth has not attempted to account for this phenomenon, which, however, is quite susceptible of explanation. A line dropped from an elevation of 25,000 feet, perpendicularly to the surface of the earth (or sea), would form the perpendicular of a right-angled triangle, of which the base would extend from the right angle to the horizon, and the hypothenuse from the horizon to the balloon. But the 25,000 feet of altitude is little or nothing, in comparison with the extent of the prospect. In other words, the base and hypothenuse of the supposed triangle would be so long when compared with the perpendicular, that the two former may be regarded as nearly parallel. In this manner the horizon of the æronaut would appear to be *on a level* with the car. But, as the point immediately beneath him seems, and is, at a great distance below him, it seems, of course, also, at a great distance below the horizon. Hence the impression of *concavity*; and this impression must remain, until the elevation shall bear so great a proportion to the extent of prospect, that the apparent parallelism of the base and hypothenuse disappears—when the earth's real convexity must become apparent.

This retraction was printed in The Sun on 15th April, 1844:

BALLOON – The mails from the South last Saturday night not having brought a confirmation of the arrival of the Balloon from England, the particulars of which from our correspondent we detailed in our Extra, we are inclined to believe that the intelligence is erroneous. The description of the Balloon and the voyage was written with a minuteness and scientific ability calculated to obtain credit everywhere, and was read with great pleasure and satisfaction. We by no means think such a project impossible.

A satirical political cartoon from Italy (1880)

NADAR

This rather comical illustration is a depiction of French photographer, caricaturist, journalist, novelist, and balloonist, Nadar (pseudonym of Gaspard-Fèlix Tournachon). Nadar (1820-1910) was the first person to take aerial photographs and also pioneered the use of artificial lighting in photography. His notoriety as an aeronaut is due to the enormous balloon he commissioned Eugène Godard to build in 1863. This leviathan, Le Gèant (The Giant), was 196 ft high and had a capacity of 210,000 cu ft, and was so impressive that it inspired Jules Verne to write 'Five Weeks in a Balloon'.

The first ascent of Le Gèant was not a complete success (having to descend after travelling a very short distance) but the second ascent was a complete disaster. The balloon took off from Champ de Mars,

Paris, on the 18th October 1863, in the presence of Napoleon III. The Gèant rose majestically and all was going well until Nadar thought he saw the sea. To avoid the waves, the balloon was abandoned to the wind – against the protest of some of the passengers. The wind was fierce and the cord to the valve broke. The younger of the Godard brothers, Jules, bravely climbed up to make a cut in the side of the balloon and the Gèant descended to the ground about 400 miles from Paris. The voyage however, was not over. The Gèant was dragged along the ground by strong winds, cutting down trees, and seriously injuring some of the passengers. Nadar himself dislocated both legs. The balloon eventually came to rest in Hanover where the blind king treated them with great hospitality. On his return to Paris, Nadar was received as a hero and continued with his aeronautical adventures. He was a forward thinking aviator and realised the limitations of balloon travel, becoming president of "The Society for the Encouragement of Aerial Locomotion by Means of Heavier than Air Machines" with Jules Verne acting as the organisation's secretary. The Gèant went on to be exhibited at the Crystal Palace in London.

An illustration of the Gèant's crash landing on its second ascent.

STEERING BALLOONS

By R. M. Ballantyne from *Up in the Clouds* (1869)

From very early on in the history of aeronautics it was realised that navigation was a crucial problem to overcome if the conquest of the skies were truly to be achieved. Many inventors modelled their theories on a method of transportation they already knew a lot about, sailing. They developed masts, sails, and rudders, but none attained the desired result. The passage below explains why.

The fallacy here may be easily pointed out. A ship is driven through water by a body in motion, namely, wind, while its rudder is dragged through a body comparatively at rest, namely, water; hence the rudder slides against or is pushed against the water, and according as it is *turned* to one side or the other, it is *pushed* to one side or the other, the stern of the ship going along with it, and the bow, of course, making a corresponding motion in the opposite direction. Thus the ship is turned or "steered," but it is manifest that if the ship were at rest there would be no pushing of the rudder by the water—no steering. On the other hand, if, though the ship were in motion, the sea was also flowing at the *same rate* with the wind, there would be no flowing of water past the ship, the rudder would not be acted on, and the vessel could not be steered.

Now a balloon, carried by the wind, cannot be steered by a rudder, because it does not, like the ship, rest half in one medium which is in motion, and half in another medium which is at rest. There is no sliding of any substance past its side, no possibility therefore of pushing a rudder against anything. All floats along *with* the wind.

If, however, the balloon could be made to go *faster* than the wind, then steering would at once become possible; but sails cannot accomplish this, because, although wind can drive a ship faster than water flows, wind cannot drive a substance faster than itself flows.

The men of old did not, however, seem to take these points into consideration. It yet remains to be seen whether steam shall ever be successfully applied to aerial machines, but this may certainly be assumed in the meantime, that, until by some means a balloon is propelled *faster than the wind* through the atmosphere, sails will be useless, and steering, or giving direction, impossible.

An illustration of Monsier Petin's gigantic aerial ship (C.1850).

The French balloonist's design utilised four balloons, "each of which should have the diameter of the Corn Exchange in Paris," supporting an aerial promenade instead of enclosed cabins. Although the ship was never constructed, due to Petin being refused funds by the French government, he had come up with an interesting solution to the problem of steering. He designed a mechanism that was like a cross between a propeller and a Venetian blind, which could be opened and closed to catch the wind and steer the ship.

THE EXPERIMENTS
OF M. HENRY GIFFARD

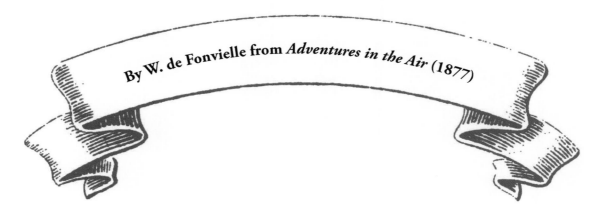

By W. de Fonvielle from *Adventures in the Air* (1877)

It was not until 1852, when Henri Giffard invented the steam injector and powered airship, that steerable flight became possible and the prospect of a reliable means of transportation was realised. The forerunner of the mighty Zeppelin, Giffard's airship disposed of all the decorative and unnecessary tackle that had previously adorned balloons, and focussed on a stripped down practical approach to flight. Nearly sixty years after the human race had first risen in to the air, powered flight had arrived, and although the airship was not the long term solution to controllable flight, it was an important step in its development.

M. Henry Giffard, who has acquired a special position in connection with aeronautics, was born at Paris in 1825, and studied at the Bourbon College. He belongs to the generation that saw the birth of railways at Paris, which took place just as he reached the age of reason. Thus the steam-locomotive, to which he has made the important addition known as Giflfard's Injector, has always exercised an invincible attraction over his mind.. Attached as a designer to the offices of the Saint-Germain and Versailles Railway, he loved, when his work was done, to mount upon the engines. The whistle was music to him, and he delighted to feel the wind in his face on a train running at full speed. He seems to have got tired, however, of this sensation, and became ambitious of experiencing that of the traveller in the air.

We may say that M. Giffard is the first inventor of a system of balloon direction who has understood the difficulty of the problem to be solved, and who has applied scientifically to his apparatus all the principles of physics and mechanics with which his education and pursuits have familiarised him. He felt that fancy ought to be rigidly banished from aerial constructions, that the form of every bit of tackle, the weight of the envelope and its resistance ought to be calculated as rigorously as if he had to do with a sheet of iron intended for the construction of an engine-boiler.

Henri Giffard (1825-1882)

Before making his experiments, M. Giffard, like a genuine engineer, began by familiarising himself with the aerial medium, and made not less than ten ascents at the Paris Hippodrome, at first along with M. Eugene Godard. Sometimes he set out alone, to the great displeasure of the professional balloonists, who played him more than one trick. One day, when he wished to open the valve, he found the lids bad been nailed. Happily the wind was light, and no accident occurred when the balloon, exhausted by the escape of gas, reached the earth.

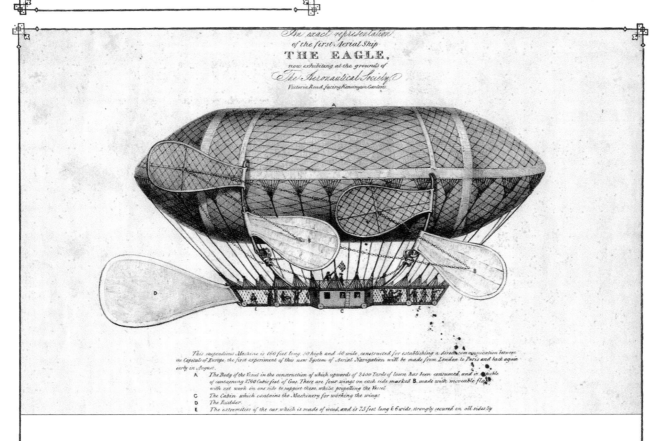

This is an illustration of an early Giffard design called "The Eagle." The craft was built but never flown. It resided at an exhibition in London until it escaped and burst.

This poster depicts Giffard's captive balloon to advertise balloon ascensions at the 1878 world's fair.

Giffard's Airship.

It was on September 24, 1852, in presence of a numerous public, that M. Giffard ascended in a steam balloon about 140 feet long, 40 feet broad, and 88,292 cubic feet in capacity. The machine, with its water and its coke for fuel, weighed in all less than 4 cwt. The engine had a force of three-horse power, and moved, at the rate of 110 revolutions per minute, a screw of three blades 10 feet in diameter.

As the inventor thought the experiment too dangerous to risk the life of another, he determined to ascend alone, and thus was enabled to take with him a larger quantity of coke and water. Thus, then, sitting in his machine with imperturbable coolness, Giffard struggled against a wind so violent that a steamer would have fled before the storm. The screw in turning produced a deep sound, and the material of the balloon swelled out under the effort. The cords attached to the balloon inclined to one side, and the aerostat itself veered round each time that the aeronaut moved his rudder.

Enthusiastic at this attempt, the value of which was increased by the memories of Pilâtre and Zambeccari, M. Emile de Girardin, who was present at the ascent, published next day in the *Presse* an article urging the Government to advance a million francs for the purpose of speedily solving the problem of aerial navigation. In vain, however; though had the future been foreseen, France might have felt it to be her interest to carry balloons to the greatest perfection possible. As M. Giffard did not return to the spot from which he started, the experiment was considered a failure. This memorable ascent ended at Trappes, where M. Giffard, owing to the darkness, was obliged to land.

M. Giffard had a contract with M. Amaud for twelve experiments which promised advantageous results. But the days were getting shorter, and the gas company feared they would not be able to supply both the Hippodrome and their regular customers; thus the experiments so well begun had to be dropped.

As we have already said, we owe to M. Giffard a magnificent invention—the Injector; an invention which will perpetuate his name, and which has brought him a fortune of several million francs. Absorbed in completing this invention, and in a multitude of researches of various kinds, it was only after several years he was able to resume his aeronautical studies.

The great obstacle which paralyzes the development of these rational attempts is that, properly speaking, there is no aerial industry. We may admit, in fact, that directable balloons might compete in speed, without difficulty, with trans-Atlantic steamers or railways, but what incredible difficulties would it be necessary to overcome in order to obtain that measure of regularity without which the carrying trade is a chimera? But even if this obstacle were overcome, it is very doubtful if the timid public could ever be induced to renounce railways and steamers for an aerial conveyance.

Meantime, he who will discover a means of exploring the air as easily as is now the case with the depths of the sea, will alone give to aerial navigation the practical—shall we say commercial?—character which it still wants, notwithstanding the results of the aerial post during the siege of Paris. It is this new service which M. Giffard has sought to render to aerial navigation since the Paris Exhibition of 1867.

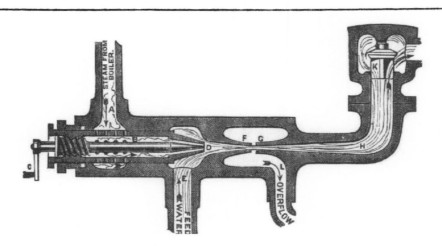

Diagram of a steam injector that Giffard invented in 1858.
A- Steam from boiler, B- Needle valve, C- Needle valve handle, D- Steam and water combine,
E- Water feed, F- Combining cone, G- Delivery nozzle and cone, H- delivery chamber and pipe,
K- Check valve, L- Overflow.

This image depicts Gaston Tissandier's airship in 1883. Fitted with a Siemens motor, it achieved the first electric-powered flight.

A poster advertising the demonstration of an early design for an airship.

An advertisement for the exhibition of a steam powered airship designed by Camille Vert at the Palais de l'industrie, séances expérimentales in Paris (c.1859).

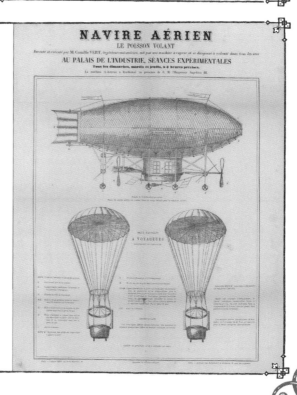

"THE BALLOON WEDDING"

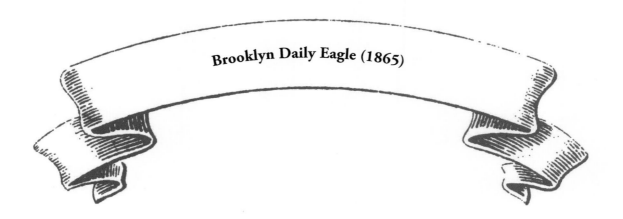

Brooklyn Daily Eagle (1865)

The following article was printed in "The Brooklyn Daily Eagle" on 9th November 1865. The idea of getting married in a balloon was quite a novelty, but apparently, if this article is anything to go by, not a novelty to be admired.

"The balloon wedding came off yesterday according to announcement, and appears to have been a rather comical affair. The bridegroom was a fat old widower of about 50, his bride a lady of 25. There was some difficulty about gas inflating the balloon, which delayed the ascension, and the public are informed that Professor Lowe had to 'make his own gas,' a feat he is very competent to perform. Owing to the deficiency of the gas, or the weight of the bridegroom, the regular bridesmaid (a stepdaughter of the bride) could not be taken up, and a lighter damsel had to be substituted.

The marriage ceremony was not performed up in the air, the officiating clergyman objecting to venture in the flesh so near Heaven. The marriage was done on terra firma, only the marriage contract was to be signed in mid-air. The balloon ascended from Central Park, in the presence of a group of gaping idlers, who amused themselves with making vulgar remarks and jokes at the expense of the bride and groom. The party descended in Yonkers in half-frozen condition. The affair would have been simply ridiculous were it not for the association with a holy ordinance which made the exhibition disgusting to every right-minded person; but as there were none such present on the occasion, excepting, perhaps, for reporters, no feelings may have been outraged."

This Belgian poster shows an air station suspended by a captive balloon at the 1894 world's fair in Antwerp.

An advertisement for a ballooning and parachuting demonstration by Eugène Godard in 1885.

SAUVETAGE DU BALLON · LE TRICOLORE ·

Monte par Monsieur et Madame DURUOF naufrages sur les cotes d'Angleterre,
et recueillis par le Patron WILLIAM OXLEY et son Second du Port de GRIMSBY le 1ᵉʳ Septembre 1874.

This is a painting of an incident in which Claude-Jules Duruof, an experienced aeronaut and instrumental pioneer in the use of balloons during the Siege of Paris, took off from Calais with his wife. The conditions were unfavourable and he had been warned against making the Channel crossing. He did not heed the advice and the couple crashed into the sea, luckily to be rescued by a passing English fisherman.

This illustration is of a single-person 'Saddle Balloon', designed by German Engineer George Rodek (C.1895). Rodek actually built this device and ascended with it, but, although novel, his invention did not catch on.

S. A. ANDRÉE'S ARCTIC BALLOON EXPEDITION OF 1897

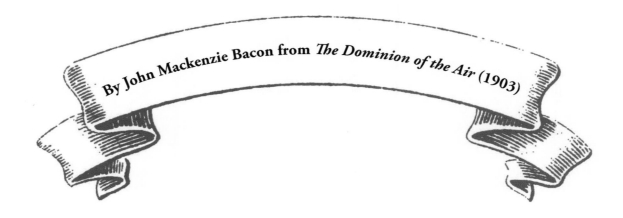

By John Mackenzie Bacon from *The Dominion of the Air* (1903)

During the 19th century, numerous attempts were made to reach the North Pole, but all failed, with many ending in disaster. None of these, however, were attempted in a balloon. A Swedish engineer named Salomon August Andrèe took up the challenge, and funded by the Royal Swedish Academy of Sciences, and notable individuals such as King Oscar II and Alfred Nobel, had a hydrogen balloon built for an aeronautical expedition to the Pole. There was great interest in this daring project, and when the Örnen ("Eagle") finally launched on 11th July 1897, it seemed like the solution to reaching the Pole had been found. This did not turn out to be the case and like so many others before them, he and his companions were lost to the icy wilderness.

Andree's grand scheme was to convey a suitable balloon, with means for inflating it, as also all necessary equipment, as far towards the Pole as a ship could proceed, and thence, waiting for a favourable wind, to sail by sky until the region of the Pole should be crossed, and some inhabited country reached beyond. The balloon was to be kept near the earth, and steered, as far as this might be practicable, by means of a trail rope. The balloon, which had a capacity of nearly 162,000 cubic feet, was made in Paris, and was provided with a rudder sail and an arrangement whereby the hang of the trail rope could be readily shifted to different positions on the ring. Further, to obviate unnecessary diffusion and loss of gas at the mouth, the balloon was fitted with a lower valve, which would only open at a moderate pressure, namely, that of four inches of water.

All preparations were completed by the summer of 1896, and on June 7th the party embarked at Gothenburg with all necessaries on board, arriving at Spitzbergen on June 21st. Andree, who was to be accompanied on his aerial voyage by two companions, M. Nils Strindberg and Dr. Ekholm, spent

S. A. Andrée
(1854–97)

Henri Lachambre's balloon workshop in Paris
where Andrée's polar balloon was made.

some time in selecting a spot that would seem suitable for their momentous start, and this was finally found on Dane's Island, where their cargo was accordingly landed.

The first operation was the erection of a wooden shed, the materials for which they had brought with them, as a protection from the wind. It was a work which entailed some loss of time, after which the gas apparatus had to be got into order, so that, in spite of all efforts, it was the 27th of July before the balloon was inflated and in readiness.

A member of an advance party of an eclipse expedition arriving in Spitzbergen at this period, and paying a visit to Andree for the purpose of taking him letters, wrote:—"We watched him deal out the letters to his men. They are all volunteers and include seven sea captains, a lawyer, and other people some forty in all. Andree chaffed each man to whom he gave a letter, and all were as merry as crickets over the business.... We spent our time in watching preparations. The vaseline (for soaking the guide ropes) caught fire to-day, but, luckily no rope was in the pot."

But the wind as yet was contrary, and day after day passed without any shift to a favourable quarter, until the captain of the ship which had conveyed them was compelled to bring matters to an issue by saying that they must return home without delay if he was to avoid getting frozen in for the winter. The balloon had now remained inflated for twenty-one days, and Dr. Ekholm, calculating that the leakage of gas amounted to nearly 1 per cent. per day, became distrustful of the capability of such a vessel to cope with such a voyage as had been aimed at. The party had now no choice but to return home with their balloon, leaving, however, the shed and gas-generating apparatus for another occasion.

This occasion came the following summer, when the dauntless explorers returned to their task, leaving Gothenburg on May 28th, 1897, in a vessel lent by the King of Sweden, and reaching Dane's Island on the 30th of the same month. Dr. Ekholm had retired from the enterprise, but in his place

From the Illustrated London News *dated 1880. This shows a proposed method of reaching the Pole by balloon, 17 years before Andrèe's expedition.*

were two volunteers, Messrs. Frankel and Svedenborg, the latter as "odd man," to fill the place of any of the other three who might be prevented from making the final venture.

It was found that the shed had suffered during the winter, and some time was spent in making the repairs and needful preparation, so that the month of June was half over before all was in readiness for the inflation. This operation was then accomplished in four days, and by midnight of June 22nd the balloon was at her moorings, full and in readiness; but, as in the previous year, the wind was contrary, and remained so for nearly three weeks. This, of course, was a less serious matter, inasmuch as the voyagers were a month earlier with their preparation, but so long a delay must needs have told prejudicially against the buoyancy of the balloon, and Andree is hardly to be blamed for having, in the end, committed himself to a wind that was not wholly favourable.

The wind, if entirely from the right direction, should have been due south, but on July 11th it had veered to a direction somewhat west of south, and Andree, tolerating no further delay, seized this as his best opportunity, and with a wind "whistling through the woodwork of the shed and flapping the canvas," accompanied by Frankel and Svedenborg, started on his ill-fated voyage.

A telegram which Andree wrote for the Press at that epoch ran thus:— "At this moment, 2.30 p.m., we are ready to start. We shall probably be driven in a north-north-easterly direction."

On July 22nd a carrier pigeon was recovered by the fishing boat Alken between North Cape, Spitzbergen, and Seven Islands, bearing a message, "July 13th, 12.30 p.m., 82 degrees 2 minutes north lat., 15 degrees 5 minutes east long. Good journey eastward. All goes well on board. Andree."

Not till August 31st was there picked up in the Arctic zone a buoy, which is preserved in the Museum of Stockholm. It bears the message, "Buoy No. 4. First to be thrown out. 11th July, 10 p.m., Greenwich mean time. All well up till now. We are pursuing our course at an altitude of about 250 metres Direction at first northerly 10 degrees east; later; northerly 45 degrees east. Four carrier pigeons were despatched at 5.40 p.m. They flew westwards. We are now above the ice, which is very cut up in all directions. Weather splendid. In excellent spirits.—Andree, Svedenborg, Frankel. (Postscript later on.) Above the clouds, 7.45, Greenwich mean time."

According to Reuter, the Anthropological and Geological Society at Stockholm received the following telegram from a ship owner at Mandal:—"Captain Hueland, of the steamship Vaagen who arrived there on Monday morning, reports that when off Kola Fjord, Iceland, in 65 degrees 34 minutes north lat., 21 degrees 28 minutes west long., on May 14th he found a drifting buoy, marked 'No. 7.' Inside the buoy was a capsule marked 'Andree's Polar Expedition,' containing a slip of paper, on which was given the following: 'Drifting Buoy No. 7. This buoy was thrown out from Andree's balloon on July 11th 1897, 10.55 p.m., Greenwich mean time, 82 degrees north lat., 25 degrees east lon. We are at an altitude of 600 metres. All well.—Andree, Svedenborg, Frankel.'"

Commenting on the first message, Mr. Percival Spencer says:—"I cannot place reliance upon the accuracy of either the date or else the lat. and long. given, as I am confident that the balloon would have travelled a greater distance in two days." It should be noted that Dane's Island lies in 79 degrees 30 minutes north lat. and 10 degrees 10 minutes east long.

Mr. Spencer's opinion, carefully considered and expressed eighteen months afterwards, will be read with real interest:—

"The distance from Dane's Island to the Pole is about 750 miles, and to Alaska on the other side about 1,500 miles. The course of the balloon, however, was not direct to the Pole, but towards Franz Josef Land (about 600 miles) and to the Siberian coast (another 800 miles). Judging from the description of the wind at the start, and comparing it with my own ballooning experience, I estimate its speed as 40 miles per hour, and it will, therefore, be evident that a distance of 2,000 miles would be covered in 50 hours, that is two days and two hours after the start. I regard all theories as to the balloon being capable of remaining in the air for a month as illusory. No free balloon has ever remained aloft for more than 36 hours, but with the favourable conditions at the northern regions (where the sun does not set and where the temperature remains equable) a balloon might remain in the air for double the length of time which I consider ample for the purpose of Polar exploration."

A record of the direction of the wind was made after Andree's departure, and proved that there was a fluctuation in direction from S.W. to N.W., indicating that the voyagers may have been borne across towards Siberia. This, however, can be but surmise. All aeronauts of experience know that it is an exceedingly difficult manoeuvre to keep a trail rope dragging on the ground if it is desirable to prevent contact with the earth on the one hand, or on the other to avoid loss of gas. A slight increase of temperature or drying off of condensed moisture may—indeed, is sure to after a while—lift the rope off the ground, in which case the balloon, rising into upper levels, may be borne away on currents which may be of almost any direction, and of which the observer below may know nothing.

The Ibsjorn Expedition which discovered the bodies of Andrée and his companions on White Island, near Spitzbergen.

This photograph of Andrèe was taken moments before the fateful ascent.

As to the actual divergence from the wind's direction which a trail rope and side sail might be hoped to effect, it may be confidently stated that, notwithstanding some wonderful accounts that have gone abroad, it must not be relied on as commonly amounting to much more than one or, at the most, two points.

Although it is to be feared that trustworthy information as to the ultimate destination of Andree's balloon may never be gained, yet we may safely state that his ever famous, though regrettable, voyage was the longest in duration ever attained. At the end of 48 hours his vessel would seem to have been still well up and going strong. The only other previous voyage that had in duration of travel approached this record was that made by M. Mallet, in 1892, and maintained for 36 hours. Next we may mention that of M. Herve, in 1886, occupying 24 1/2 hours, which feat, however, was almost equal led by the great Leipzig balloon in 1897, which, with eight people in the car, remained up for 24 1/4 hours, and did not touch earth till 1,032 miles had been traversed.

The fabric of Andree's balloon may not be considered to have been the best for such an exceptional purpose. Dismissing considerations of cost, goldbeaters' skin would doubtless have been more suitable. The military balloons at Aldershot are made of this, and one such balloon has been known to remain inflated for three months with very little loss. It is conceivable, therefore, that the chances of the voyagers, whose ultimate safety depended so largely upon the staying power of their aerial vessel, might have been considerably increased.

One other expedient, wholly impracticable, but often seriously discussed, may be briefly referred to, namely, the idea of taking up apparatus for pumping gas into metal receivers as the voyage proceeds, in order to raise or lower a balloon, and in this way to prolong its life. Mr. Wenham has investigated the point with his usual painstaking care, and reduced its absurdity to a simple calculation, which should serve to banish for good such a mere extravagant theory.

Suppose, he says, the gas were compressed to one-twentieth part of its bulk, which would mean a pressure within its receiver of 300 lbs. per square inch, and that each receiver had a capacity of 1 cubic foot, while for safety sake it was made of steel plates one-twentieth of an inch thick, then each receiver would weigh 10 lbs., and to liberate 1,000 feet clearly a weight of 500 lbs. would have to be taken up. Now, when it is considered that 1,000 cubic feet of hydrogen will only lift 72 lbs., the scheme begins to look hope less enough. But when the question of the pumping apparatus, to be worked by hand, is contemplated the difficulties introduced become yet more insuperable. The only feasible suggestion with respect the use of compressed gas is that of taking on board charged cylinders under high pressure, which, after being discharged to supply the leakage of the balloon could, in an uninhabited country, be cast out as ballast last. It will need no pointing out, however, that such an idea would be practically as futile as another which has gravely been recommended, namely, that of heating the gas of the balloon by a Davy lamp, so as to increase its buoyancy at will. Major Baden-Powell has aptly described this as resembling "an attempt to warm a large hall with a small spirit lamp."

In any future attempt to reach the Pole by balloon it is not unreasonable to suppose that wireless telegraphy will be put in practice to maintain communication with the base. The writer's personal experience of the possibilities afforded by this mode of communication, yet in its infancy, will be given.

A captive balloon aloft above the Eiffel tower in Paris. Watercolour over graphite by Camille Grávis.

THE MILITARY APPLICATIONS OF BALLOONING

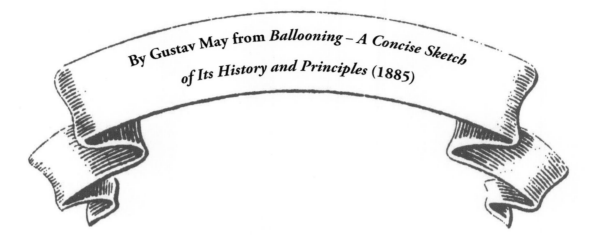

By Gustav May from *Ballooning – A Concise Sketch of Its History and Principles* (1885)

It has rarely taken long for the human race to adapt any new technology into a tool of war, and the balloon was no exception. Only a decade after the first demonstrations by professor Charles, hydrogen balloons were used by the French military to spy on the Austrian army during the Battle of Fleurus (1794). As an observation tool they were effective, but as you will see, early attempts to weaponize them were not quite as successful. Probably the most impressive use of balloons during war was that of the brave aeronauts who 'escaped the Seige of Paris (1870-1871) when 70 balloons' soared over the Prussian forces to reopen lines of communication with the rest of France. Balloons, such as barrage balloons used to obstruct air attacks, continued to be used for war in the 20th century, but their role in reconnaissance was largley given over to the more versatile aeroplane.

The first movement attempted to turn aeronautics into an aid for military operations was made by the French government in 1794. The author of this movement may be accepted in the person of a celebrated chemist, Guyten de Merveau, then a member of the National Convention. He proposed to employ balloons, held captive by cords, and in the boat attached to place some competent person to watch the position and movements of the enemy. The proposition was approved by the Comitè de Salut, and the first preparations were instituted by Guyten de Merveau and another eminent chemist, Coutelle, who had now joined him in this enterprise. Coutelle, began the preparation of the gas, hydrogen, with a furnace, in which he put a cast iron tube, three feet long and fourteen inches in diameter, which he filled with one hundredweight of sheet-iron clippings. This tube was terminated at each of its extremities by an iron pipe. One of them served to conduct the current of steam, which was decomposed by the contact of the heated metal, the other directed into the balloon the hydrogen resulting from this decomposition.

By reason of many accidents the operation was very long, yet there was obtained five hundred and

Aerostatic Corps balloon during the Battle of Fleurus.

fifty cubic feet of gas. The government commission was satisfied with this result and Coutelle received orders to proceed to Belgium and to submit to General Jourdain the proposition to apply balloons to the operations of his army. His opinion was at once favourable. The Republic then founded the Institution of Military Aeronautics, and Coutelle was nominated director of aeronautic experiments, and he established himself in the garden of the little Chateau de Meudon, and connected the scientist, Jacques Contè with his labours.

They constructed a silk balloon calculated to carry two persons, and arranged for the filling a new furnace in which were placed seven cast iron tubes. These tubes, nine yards and a quarter long altogether, and the same measurement as previously in diameter, were each filled with four hundred and fifty pounds of iron clippings, which were crushed with a rammer into the tubes. The gas was thus easily and abundantly obtained. One and a half pint of water furnished three cubic feet of hydrogen and only twelve to fifteen hours were necessary to fill the balloon.

The great difficulty was to prevent the hydrogen from escaping through the silk envelope of the balloon. If there had been a necessity for the preparation of gas and filling the balloon every two or three days in the midst of military operations the system would have been impracticable, so that it was important to have the material of the aerial vessel impervious; an advance in the art not then attained.

This problem, until then not solved, was decided by the chemists Coutelle and Contè, so that they were enabled to retain the hydrogen in the balloon two months, and frequently at the Meudon School the balloons were sometimes three months full of gas.

The incorporation of the Corps of Aeronautics (Compagnie d'Aerostiers) was followed by great activity at several military operations, in aerially reconnoitring the position and movements of the enemy. Conveying the balloon filled from place to place was a work of much difficulty and, at times, of damage to the air craft itself. For this work seventeen men were sometimes told off, each holding one of the ropes, about thirty feet long, hanging down from the balloon, and so drawing it along, very often over serious impediments.

An illustration of a plan by the British to utilise a tethered balloon to remotely release dynamite above the enemy position.

This body always followed the march of the army. Without going over the various incidents of their employment, it may be sufficient to state that after a career of usefulness mixed with some failures, Napoleon, who does not seem to have been much enamoured of aeronautics for military purposes, ordered the school at Meudon to be closed, and all the material to be sold.

Since that period the balloon has been employed by several governments in their war operations, to reconnoitre the position and movements of the enemy. By Russia in 1812, and Austria in 1849, before Venice; and by Napoleon III. in his Italian campaign, preceding the battle of Solferino.

First Military Balloon, Fleurus 1794.

The first air raids in history at the Siege of Venice, 15th July, 1849.

After the Republic of San Marco was formed, following a revolt in Venice against Austrian rule, the Austrians retaliated and besieged the city, using balloons as a method of delivering bombs. The concept was pioneered by Austrian artillery lieutenant Franz von Uchatius who developed small unmanned paper balloons that could carry bombs released by a time fuse. However, the wind proved unpredictable and the attack relatively ineffective, with some of the balloons even blowing over Venice and falling on the Austrian army. The following article is from the Morning Chronicle *newspaper on 29th August 1849, and reports the use of these balloons a week after Venice surrendered to the Austrians on 22nd August.*

"The Soldaten Freund publishes a letter from the artillery officer Uchatius, who first proposed to subdue Venice by ballooning. From this it appears that the operations were suspended for want of a proper vessel exclusively adapted for this mode of warfare, as it became evident, after a few experiments had been made, that, as the wind blows nine times out of ten from the sea, the balloon inflation must be conducted on board ship; and this was the case on July the 15th, the occasion alluded to in a former letter, when two balloons armed with shrapnels ascended from the deck of the Volcano war steamer, and attained a distance of 3,500 fathoms in the direction of Venice; and exactly at the moment calculated upon, i. e., at the expiration of twenty-three minutes, the explosion took place. The captain of the English brig Frolic, and other persons then at Venice, testify to the extreme terror and the morale effect produced on the inhabitants.

A stop was put to further exhibitions of this kind by the necessity of the Vulcan going into docks to undergo repairs, which the writer regrets the more, as the currents of wind were for a long time favourable to his schemes. One thing is established beyond all doubt (he adds), viz., that bombs and other projectiles can be thrown from balloons at a distance of 5,000 fathoms, always provided the wind be favourable."

But the greatest employment of aeronautics, in modem days, was made by France when Paris was besieged in 1870-1871 by the German army. It is known how, during the siege of Paris, intelligence was carried by means of balloons, over the heads of the enemy, and through carrier pigeons the state of the city was transmitted throughout the provinces. The size of the balloons employed were generally of 2000 cb.m. volume, although other sizes were constructed down to 700 cb.m. The first balloon ascended on the 23rd of September, 1870, the last on the 28th of January, 1871. Altogether sixty-four balloons left Paris; five fell into the hands of the Germans, two were carried to sea. These made the ascent at night, and at day- break were over the ocean, but by unfavourable atmospheric currents were carried on to land again; one reached as far as Christiana in Norway, doing the journey in fifteen hours. One of the sixty-four balloons was furnished with a steering apparatus, but the propeller screw was powerless to resist the atmospheric pressure upon the great surface of the balloon; it fell, after a seven hours' journey, in the department of Marne, far from its destined landing-place. Of all these sixty-four balloons not one succeeded in re-entering Paris, although many ingenious contrivances were suggested for that important object. Manifestly science was taxed to the utmost to discover a means of attaining so vital an advantage to the French people, and in its failure to do so,

A balloon in the distance during the Siege of Paris (1870-1871).

During the American Civil War (1861-1865) balloons were used for aerial reconnaissance and artillery spotting. On one occasion in 1862, military legend George Armstrong Custer ascended with Thaddeus Lowe, a seasoned aeronaut. Custer was initially apprehensive but his nerves settled and he went on to make many ascents in observation balloons.

'Previous to this time I had never even seen a balloon except from a distance. Being interested in their construction, I was about to institute a thorough examination of all its parts, when the aeronaut announced that all was ready. He inquired whether I desired to go up alone, or he should accompany me. My desire, if frankly expressed, would have been not to go up at all; but if I was to go, company was certainly desirable. With an attempt at indifference, I intimated that he might go along.'

– George Armstrong Custer

we may read the prominent weak point in aeronautics. During this memorable siege, the Academy of Sciences were overwhelmed with letters containing offers of inventions for steering balloons, but without any corroborative proof, by actual experiments, of the practicability of the writers' inventions or plans.

However, as Dupuy do Lôme, member of the Academy, was in possession, as he thought, of a process by which this important object was attainable, he was commissioned by the Academy, and funds supplied him, to test his method.

The aerial vessel adapted by him was in reality but little different from that of Mr. Henry Giffard. The difference lies in the latter having a steam engine, whilst Dupuy, who feared the vicinity of a furnace near inflammable gas, was content with manual force. This idea of Dupuy de Lôme came to nothing, as the war was ended before his procrastinated plans were put into practice.

It is interesting to note the direction in the flight of the balloons despatched from Paris during the siege.

They were generally sent off in couples, within a few minutes or an hour or two of each other. Taking eight couples so sent off, we find,

1 fell at Montdierdia			1 fell at Cremery		
1	„	Nugent Aube	1	„	Britton Meuse
1	„	Vignoles	1	„	Verdun
1	„	Loire Inferieure	1	„	Eare et Loire
1	„	Ferrières	1	„	Vitry
1	„	Holland	1	„	Norway
1 fell into the sea and					
was impelled on shore			1	„	Brittany
again by a change of wind					
1 fell at Somme			1	„	Cremery.

On the value of balloons, as so-called captive balloons, for military operations, opinions are somewhat divided. There are many difficulties in the way of their successful employment, commensurate with the cost and labour engaged in organising an adequate staff for them, and providing the necessary suitable gas to fill them.

It is probable that the opposed opinions of military men have been formed from accidental differences, arising from the state of the weather, or other causes when they have been personally engaged with the captive balloon for reconnoitring; although un- favourable opinions are entertained by distinguished military men, as to the general employment of the captive balloon for military purposes, yet it is on record that in modem days many signal advantages have been obtained by its use during war. Napoleon III. owed much of his success in his Italian campaign to it. Nadar and Godard were engaged to make a recognisance of the enemy's position previous to the battle of Solferino, and the knowledge thus gained was of essential benefit to the French army. At the battle of Richmond, the North Americans undoubtedly owed their success greatly to the reconnoitring, assisted by a Morse telegraphic apparatus from the aerial craft in connection with the balloon station; the captive balloon being secured by a rope of three hundred to nine hundred feet long. Once, when General Porter was observing the movements of the enemy from a captive balloon, the cable broke and he found himself floating towards the Confederate Army. He at once took measures for making the balloon descend, and fortunately for him it struck a current of air going in the opposite direction, and landed him safely among his own people. During the two days' fighting at Fair Oaks, Mr. Lowe watched the battle from a height two thousand feet, and was the first to make known the general retreat of the enemy.

A great difficulty in the employment of the balloon for military purposes lies in the production of the necessary gas, which has to be renewed often, and therefore requires an apparatus which must follow the troops wherever they go, so as to have the gas at hand. As it is seldom that balloon stations are in the vicinity of gas works, and as the transport of coal gas in suitable vessels is difficult, even when the vessels are closed with care, hydrogen is preferred. In England the apparatus for gas making for military operations, does not generally exceed six tons in weight, and for the purpose of easy carriage, no part exceeds six hundredweight.

Such apparatus produces per hour some four hundred and thirty cubic feet of gas, and fills a balloon of moderate size in three or four hours. For its production a combustible material on the spot is available. In the defence of fortresses the employment of coal gas is mostly the case; with sieges, however, as in field campaigns, hydrogen is almost exclusively used.

We may assume that in sieges when the nature of the ground permits, ascents at night are practicable, and in the boat of a balloon a concave mirror may be placed for electrical illumination, by means of which the ground is inspected and the works of the enemy reconnoitred. The electric apparatus remains on the ground, and an insulated copper wire in the rope of the balloon is also employed to transmit intelligence. Naturally it is better that the balloon remains in telegraphic connection in order to communicate intelligence immediately.

It is known that Prussia, in 1870, formed in Cologne, two detachments of aeronauts, comprising twenty men, in order to employ them before Strasburg. For this purpose Henry Coxwell was engaged to instruct them in a service which his great experience so well fitted him to do. After the delivery of his balloon, the work of filling with hydrogen was attempted, but owing to the violent winds, and the leakage of the conducting hose, the balloon obtained a lifting force for only one person. It certainly ascended three-hundred and fifty feet, but, owing to stormy winds, no observations were possible. The detachment was afterwards drawn to Paris, where on account of mist and other unfavourable weather no progress could be made.

The French government has instituted on several occasions inquiries for the purpose of arriving at the capabilities of the balloon for military operations. In 1871, the minister of war appointed a special commission under the presidency of Colonel Laussebet, assisted by the distinguished Captains, Renard and Delamore, for that object. The result of the commission was favourable to the re-establishment of the Aeronautic School at Meudon, abolished by Napoleon, ninety years previously, and to the formation of an efficient body of aeronauts. The commission led to important discoveries in the varnish used for the silk, so as to strengthen it against the escape of gas; also as to the facilities in landing, with other improvements in connection with captive balloons.

*Two children ascending in the basket of a balloon waving a
flag and handkerchief.*

A SUMMARY OF
THE EARLY HISTORY OF

At the beginning of the 20th century, a new technology took to the air that would revolutionise aeronautics. When the 'Wright Flyer', designed by Orville and Wilbur Wright, made its maiden flight in 1903, travelling a distance of 120 feet, it set the tone for the future of aviation. Aeroplanes proved far more useful as a method of air travel, soon developing commercial and military applications and largely relegating the balloon to scientific and recreational uses. There were still records to be set however, and brave aeronauts prepared to risk their lives to set them. For example, altitude was a domain in which the balloon outperformed the plane – the first people to reach the stratosphere doing so in a hydrogen balloon, ascending to 51,000 feet in 1931. It was also utilising a balloon, all be it a helium one, that Joseph Kittinger of the United States Air Force reached the record height of 102,800 feet in 1960. Once he achieved this staggering altitude, he then stepped out of the gondola, breaking the records for the highest parachute jump, longest drogue-fall (four minutes), and fastest speed by a human being through the atmosphere (614 mph). 52 years later he worked on the Red Bull Stratos project on which he advised skydiver Felix Baumgartner during his attempt to better his records. The project was a success; Baumgartner reached 127,851 feet before alighting and falling to earth.

Although aeroplanes had already been first past the post for many challenges, such as the trans-Atlantic and trans-Pacific crossings, the will and pioneering spirit of balloonists remained. A new era of hi-tech ballooning appeared and a new breed of aeronauts like Per Lindstrand, Steve Fosset, and Bertrand Piccard, became the Roziers and Blanchards of the late 20th Century. The oceans have now been crossed, even the entire globe has been circumnavigated, and yet the technology continues to inspire and drive innovation. For example, cluster balloonist Jonathan Trappe (where the aeronaut ascends attached to many small helium balloons) has already crossed the English Channel and attempted a trans-Atlantic voyage. He also reached an altitude of 14,783ft, while suspended under the balloons on his trademark unmodified office chair.

Ballooning developed a sporting aspect to it too. The Gordon Bennett Cup is the world's oldest gas balloon race and was first held in 1906 from Paris. Sponsored by millionaire sportsman, James Gordon Bennett Jr., the organisers say the aim of the contest "is simple: to fly the furthest distance from the launch site." The record distance for this contest is held by Wilhelm Eimers and Bernd Landsmann who in 2005 piloted their balloon 21,000 miles from their start point.

Many people all over the world now enjoy the activity as a recreational pastime, and just like at the birth of aeronautics, the spectacle of an ascending balloon still inspires awe. Balloon fiestas, such as the world's largest in Albuquerque, New Mexico, are a testament to this continuing popularity and that the romance of the pursuit is still alive and well.

I hope you have enjoyed this tour through the annals of ballooning history and that it has given you an intriguing taste of its colourful origins. Bon voyage!

Printed in Great Britain
by Amazon